SPLENDID SENIORS

Great Lives, Great Deeds

Jack Adler

PEARLSONG PRESS
NASHVILLE, TN

Pearlsong Press
P.O. Box 58065
Nashville, TN 37205
www.pearlsong.com
1-615-356-5188
1-866-4-A-PEARL

ISBN: 978-1-59719-007-7
Library of Congress Control Number: 2006938352

Cover and interior design by Zelda Pudding.

Front cover photo of Tuolumne Meadows in Yosemite National Park is courtesy
of PDPhoto.org. Other cover photographs of Mary Baker Eddy, Alexander
Graham Bell, Thurgood Marshall, Grandma Moses, Thomas Edison, John Muir, a
painting of Benjamin Franklin and a Roman bust of Sophocles are public domain
images. Edison and Franklin images are from the Library of Congress, Prints and
Photographs Division, Detroit Company Collection. Muir photograph is from the
Library of Congress, Evolution of the Conservation Movement, 1850-1920.

Dedicated to my sons,
Jason and Greg

Foreword

"*Life* *does not cease when you are old,*
it only suffers a rich change."

JANE ELLEN HARRISON
an English classical scholar/writer
who died at 78.

"*If I'd known I was gonna live this long,*
I'd have taken better care of myself."

EUBIE BLAKE
an American show business luminary,
on the occasion of his 100th birthday.

These two comments reflect the situation of seniors ("elders," "the mature," "the aged" or any similar terms) today: They are going to live longer, and the expanded chapters of their lives can be rich and fulfilling.

The attitude of society to seniors, and of seniors to themselves, has changed dramatically through the ages. The time of life when one was considered a senior has also been greatly modified. In the same vein, the amount of time one anticipated living after arriving at such an accepted but arbitrary age has also shifted. The expectations of society to what "seniors" should or could do in their "remaining time" has also undergone changes.

In bygone eras one could be considered a senior in the 40–50 range, with little expectation of making it beyond—though there were many exceptions. Less activity was expected, and it was relatively rare for someone to strike out into another field. Today, the 40–60 range in the U.S. and other well-developed countries is considered middle age, with people expecting to live another one to three decades; however, even this middle period (coined "middlescence" by some social scientists) has emerged as a period to strike out into new endeavors.

The over-85 age group is the fastest growing sector of the

American population, whereas one's 65th birthday still remains—for the most part—the marker of seniority. Life expectancy is about 76 in the U.S, the highest in history. Clearly, the amount of time one has after reaching the label of being a "senior" has risen significantly. In the same vein, many post-65 people today either retire, continue working in the same field, or seek new vistas. Coping with retirement, however, can be a daunting process for some people, especially those who aren't able to redirect their new time in satisfactory ways.

Not too many decades ago seniors dropped out of society and the economy after reaching their so-called "golden years." Seniors, for the most part, were considered to be recipients of rather than contributors to society and the economy. But today's world is vastly different.

The role of seniors, at least economically, has been dramatically redefined, which is easily understood when one realizes the 55-plus age group controls more than half of the nation's wealth. Nevertheless, health and financial security still remain among the most important concerns of seniors—but the way they handle these issues has changed, with seniors taking a far more active rather than passive approach to seek control over their lives. The same energy is also being used to generate and channel their creativity.

The purpose of this book is to illustrate what contributions to society have been made by representative famous people throughout history. What they accomplished as seniors may have been made possible or easier by their previous training and successes, but the greatest achievement, perhaps, was that they kept working and contributing and didn't surrender to their advanced age and related disabilities. The age of 65 was used as the cut-off point for inclusion in this book to adhere to an age traditionally associated with retirement from the mainstream, though it's clear that fewer people reached this age before the 20th century, and many more reach it now, in the 21st. Moreover, improved health will lessen the impact of disabilities that deter active participation in life. As life spans increase, so will the amount of time in which one can aspire to greater personal and social achievement.

This book only covers 52 personalities—one for each week in the year—although there are easily many more whose lives deserve to be described in this context.

The reality, as many discover, is that how you age and react to aging is more than physical; you are, to a considerable extent, as old as you feel and think you are. Your mind can stay relatively young and help in meaningful renewals, particularly if you're receptive to new experiences and endeavors.

Samuel Johnson, the 18ᵗʰ century London writer and wit, put it a bit harshly but well when he said: "It's a man's own fault from want of use if his mind grows torpid in old age."

Jack Adler

Table of Contents

FOREWORD   5

Sophocles   11
Michelangelo   14
Galileo   18
Isaac Newton   23
Benjamin Franklin   26
Benjamin Disraeli   31
Louis Pasteur   35
Susan Anthony   39
Henrik Ibsen   43
Leo Tolstoy   47
Mark Twain   50
Mary Baker Eddy   54
John Muir   58
Andrew Carnegie   61
Alexander Graham Bell   65
Sarah Bernhardt   70
Thomas Edison   74
Oliver Wendell Holmes   78
Sigmund Freud   82
William Butler Yeats   86
Ignace Paderewski   89
Mahatma Gandhi   93
George Bernard Shaw   97
George Santayana   101
Albert Einstein   105
Thomas Mann   110
Arturo Toscanini   114
Frank Lloyd Wright   117

Grandma Moses   122
Sir Henry Beecham   126
Eleanor Roosevelt   129
Robert Frost   133
General Douglas MacArthur   136
Winston Churchill   141
W. Somerset Maugham   144
Jean Arp   151
Le Corbusier   148
Charles de Gaulle   154
Reinhold Niebuhr   158
Igor Stravinsky   162
Pablo Picasso   165
David Ben-Gurion   168
Casey Stengel   173
Charles Chaplin   177
Margaret Mead   181
Marc Chagall   185
Andres Segovia   190
Irving Berlin   193
Thurgood Marshall   197
Jonas Salk/Albert Sabin   201
Mother Teresa   204
Benjamin Spock   208

BIBLIOGRAPHY   213

ABOUT THE AUTHOR   221

Sophocles
490–405/6 B.C.

"No man loves life
like him that is growing old."

"No falsehood
lingers on into old age."

TWO remarkable statements made by Sophocles, one of the greatest dramatists in ancient Greece, whose works are still produced today and whose comments on old age as well as life are still eminently quotable. Sophocles, during his long life, was also an actor, ordained priest, general, and a government official. Gathering philosophical strength while utilizing his diversified life experiences, Sophocles wrote some of his masterpieces after the age of 65, including *Oepidus at Colonus* at the age of 89, a year before he died around 405/6 B.C. Another classic work, *Electra,* was written when he was a mere 70.

A keen observer of Hellenic life, and consistently writing in his old age despite suffering various enfeeblements, Sophocles actually wrote over 120 plays. Only seven, however, have survived in their entirety, including such other classics as *Oedipus the King* and *Antigone.* He is also credited with making several key innovations in staging dramas: relating a story/tragedy in one play rather than the customary trilogy of the period; adding a third actor; and creating scene painting on canvas, which added to the overall impact of the production besides further developing career opportunities for scenic designers. He also helped to develop innovative mechanical devices such as a wheeled platform and means to allow a "god" to float over the stage. His central theme was that his characters could use their free will to govern their lives, but that fate still played a major role in what happened to them, with only the gods enabled to foresee the future and understand the tragic flaws of mankind.

SPLENDID SENIORS

Born in Colonus near Athens around 490–496 B.C. to a wealthy merchant family, Sophocles received a good education. His lifespan captured the rise and fall of the Athenian "Golden Age." As a good friend of the famed Athenian leader Pericles, Sophocles was close to the political scene. Though not a politician himself, he was still active in the Athenian government at the age of 83. In 413 B.C. he belonged to a committee of 10 senior citizens that ultimately implemented a temporary oligarchy over the city/state. When criticized about establishment of this oligarchy, considered a questionable move by some Athenians and a setback to their form of democracy, Sophocles argued that there was no better alternative at the time. At one point he was elected, as a measure of his stature, as one of Athens' generals, though it was recognized that he was hardly a military strategist.

Sophocles also served as an ordained priest in the service, among others, of Asclepias, the Greek god of medicine. In his early days he also performed as an actor in his own plays, but gave this up eventually, as his voice was not considered particularly strong or powerful. Voices had to carry well in the outdoor amphitheaters where the plays were normally presented.

Regardless of his vocal quality, Sophocles was considered a highly skilled writer with a remarkable ability to evoke emotions in his audiences. He had the nickname of "The Attic Bee" (Attica is the name of the geographical area Athens is in) as it was believed he was capable of distilling pure honey from words. His plays won more first prizes in the "Great Dionysia" (Dionysus was the god of fertility), an annual five day festival celebrated by the ancient Athenians, than any other dramatist.

Sophocles, by contemporary comments, was considered to be an attractive personality with good looks, wit and charm. He also had a sense of loyalty, considering that when he was well on in years he led the chorus of one of his plays onto the stage at a Great Dionysia dressed in mourning for his fellow and younger playwright, Euripides (another of the great ancient Greek dramatists); Euripides had been banished from Athens due to adverse reaction to his *The Trojan Women* (an anti-war play opposed by some Athenians). Admired by some, his stance earned Sophocles considerable enmity in other Athenian quarters.

In his old age, questions arose whether Sophocles had begun to neglect his own household because he was no longer capable of handling all the duties expected of him. Taken to court by his sons (he had several sons, legitimate and otherwise, some of whom also became playwrights), Sophocles managed to prove he wasn't senile, with his defense also featuring his recital of an ode from his own play *Oedipus at Colonus*. Obviously impressed by his performance, the court ruled in his favor.

Asked during his senior days whether he could still have sex with a woman, Sophocles replied: "Hush, my friend, I am only too grateful to have escaped from this, just as if I had escaped a crazed and savage master."

Among his other memorable lines, some from fragments of his plays, are:

"If I am Sophocles, I am not mad;
and if I am not mad, I am not Sophocles."

"One must learn by doing the thing;
for though you think you know it,
you have no certainty until you try."

"None love the messenger who brings bad news."

"Wonders are many, but none so more than man."

Michelangelo
1475–1564

"I have seen Michelangelo, although
*more than sixty years old and no longer among the most
robust, knock off more chips off a very hard marble
in a quarter of an hour than three young stone carvers
could have done in three or four..."*

So wrote a contemporary of Michelangelo when the sculptor, artist, architect and poet was already 70 and still creating one of his master-pieces. His creations, especially the expressive lines of the human form, greatly influenced other artists during his life and to this day.

Michelangelo, one of the supreme artists in history, was still carving the *Rondanini Pieta* (a "pieta" is a representation of the Virgin Mary mourning over the dead body of Christ) when he died two weeks before his 89th birthday. Having difficulty sleeping at night, he had devised a cardboard helmet holding a candle that enabled him to see the marble and to free his hands.

Keenly aware of his condition—he suffered from kidney stones—and that both life and his ability to create were coming to an end, he wrote: "Art and death do not go well together."

But he enjoyed a long and productive life. In 1542, when he was 67, he wrote in his notebook: "I am a poor man and of little worth, who is laboring in that art that God has given me in order to extend my life as long as possible."

Michelangelo, who performed commissions for many popes during a period when artists depended on patronage from the high and mighty, acquired substantial property and died a rich man. At the height of his fame his talents were also sought after by Suleiman, ruler of the Turks, King Francis of France, and the Holy Roman Emperor

Charles V.

Michelangelo was born in the Tuscany region near Florence and considered himself a "son of Florence." After some time at a workshop, he managed as a distant relative of the reigning Medici family to enter their household, where he acquired more training as an artist as well as a humanist education.

After finishing some sculptures showing his skill he went to Rome, where he created a marble pieta that brought him considerable attention. When he returned to Florence, quite famous by this time, he received a commission for a sculpture of David. His huge—over 14 feet high—rendition is considered one of the greatest works of sculpture.

In 1508 Pope Julius II summoned him to paint the ceiling of the Sistine Chapel. The work was arduous—lying on his back on scaffolding—but by 1512 he had painted more than 300 figures. In his copious notes he wrote: "After four tortured years, more than 400 over life-sized figures, I felt as old and as weary as Jeremiah. I was only 37, yet friends did not recognize the old man I had become."

And in a sonnet, one of his many poems, he penned:

And ever above my face the brush dripping,
making a rich pavement out of me,
My loins have been shoved into my guts,
My arse serves to counterweight my rump.

Other commissions—not all completed—followed. These include a tomb for Pope Julius (which had the famed figure of Moses, another of his noteworthy sculptures), the Laurentian Library in Florence, and the Medici Tombs for the new sacristy of San Lorenzo. He was even utilized as a military architect when put in charge of creating Florence's fortifications.

Of his sculpture, and how intellect and inspiration work, he wrote:

No block of marble but it does not hide
the concept living in the artist's mind—
pursuing it inside that form, he'll guide
his hand to shape what reason has defined.

He also wrote, in another sonnet, that:

The very best artist has no idea
How unlimited in itself a single block of marble is.

Pope Clement VII commissioned him in 1534 to paint the fresco of the Last Judgment in the Sistine Chapel. He finished this monumental work—the world's greatest single fresco—in 1541, just past his 65th birthday. Many of his figures were painted nude, as was his practice. The nudity upset more conservative elements of Rome. A decade later, a second artist—dubbed the "breeches-maker"—added covers to various private parts.

During his last 30 years his work was more architectural than in other fields, though he kept writing poetry. In a letter to his contemporary, Giorgio Vasari (author of *The Life of Michelangelo),* he wrote: "It is God's will, Vasari, that I should continue to live in misery for some years. I know that you will tell me that I am an old fool to wish to write sonnets, but since many say that I am in my second childhood, I have sought to act accordingly."

When a priest commented that it was a pity that he hadn't married, Michelangelo responded, "I have only too much of a wife in this art of mine, who has always kept me in tribulation, and my children shall be the works that I may leave, which, even if they are naught, will live a while."

In 1546, in his 70s, he was made—by papal demand—the chief architect of St. Peter's Basilica. Michelangelo wrote to a nephew: "Many believe—and I believe—that I have been designated for this work by God. In spite of my old age, I do not want to give it up; I work out of love for God and I put my hope in Him."

His dome for St. Peter's Basilica, his major architectural achievement, has served as a model for domes throughout the western world. Many of the state capitol buildings, as well as the Capitol in Washington D.C., are derived from Michelangelo's creation.

Even when he was 84 he was asked to work on another family papal tomb in Rome.

When the end was near, Michelangelo declared his will in three sentences, giving "his soul to God, his body to the earth, and his material possessions to his nearest relatives."

Though the pope wanted Michelangelo to be buried with honors in Rome, his family managed to smuggle his body to Florence, where Michelangelo wanted to be put to rest. His monument is at the Church of Santa Croce in Florence, where Florentines and others venerated him as a "master of all the arts."

Among Michelangelo's quotes:

"I saw the angel in the marble and carved until I set him free."

"The true work of art is but a shadow of the divine perfection."

"Lord, grant that I may always desire more than I can accomplish."

"If people knew how hard I worked to get my mastery, it wouldn't seem so wonderful at all."

"Genius is eternal patience."

Galileo Galilei
1564–1642

"In questions of science the authority of a thousand is not worth the humble reasoning of a single individual."

Galileo, who lived in what is now Italy in the 16th century, was one of the major scientific figures in history. But his discoveries and theories about the nature of the world led him into tremendous difficulties. Galileo's major accomplishments took place before he was 65, but the major dramas of his life came in his later years.

He was a key exponent in developing precise methodical experiments and measurements to establish and prove theories rather than to just accept ancient theories by Aristotle that were approved of by academicians of his time as well as by the Roman Catholic Church. Galileo lived during the early Renaissance, and his life exemplified the struggle to separate science from religion.

Galileo's own discoveries led him to become a champion of the Copernican theory, which held that the Earth revolved around the Sun and not vice-versa. This was a very controversial notion and a viewpoint disputed by many, including some members of the Roman Catholic hierarchy who felt more comfortable with the Ptolemaic version of the order of the heavens. Copernicus' opus *On the Revolutions* had been placed on the Church's "Index of Forbidden Books."

Galileo was born in Pisa in 1564. He abandoned a career in medicine begun at the University of Pisa. By this time he had demonstrated a keen intellect and interest in natural phenomena, showing a preference for mathematics and philosophy. His search for knowledge led to some difficult questions for his teachers to answer, and he acquired the nickname "the wrangler."

He went on to get a position teaching mathematics at the University of Pisa and later as the head of the mathematics department at the

University of Padua. Throughout his academic career he managed to get the support of most students but the enmity of some of his professorial peers. Some of his detractors even hissed at his lectures.

While teaching Galileo continued his experiments, succeeding in many scientific inventions and discoveries. Among his efforts he invented a thermoscope (a primitive thermometer), a mathematical instrument called a sector, a machine for raising water, and various discoveries in mathematics, physics (including disproving the Aristotelian theory on the force of gravity), and astronomy. He put together, for example, a number of telescopes—each one stronger—which helped him to discover Jupiter's satellites and that the moon, far from being a perfect sphere, was pockmarked and had phases. He also developed an early form of compass.

Though accused of being intellectually arrogant and a "cultural politician," Galileo once confessed: "The weakness of my intellect, the terror of being mistaken, has greatly confounded me."

Galileo, in his writings and letters, aroused the ire of others with his belief that science should be conducted aside from the scriptures. One illustration of his outlook was that the Bible taught "how one goes to heaven, not how heaven goes."

In 1630, when he was already 66, Galileo received conditional permission from the Church to publish his *Dialogue Concerning the Chief Systems of the World,* which covered his discoveries in astronomy and confirmed Copernicus's theory. He kept working on the book, surviving the plague that ravaged the area. In 1632 his book came out and created a sensation. However, further distribution was forbidden by church officials while a specially appointed commission assessed the book. Unfortunately for Galileo, the commission's negative report led Pope Urban VIII to refer the book to the dreaded Inquisition, whose task it was to root out what it considered heresy against the tenets of the Church.

Subsequently, Galileo was summoned from his villa at Arcetri near Florence to come to Rome. Galileo asked for the trial/hearing to be held in Florence, but the Church refused and advised him to show up or be brought to Rome in chains.

In April 1633 Galileo was formally interrogated by the Inquisition. The threat of torture was always a possibility, as this was one of the Inquisition's tools. In effect, he was allowed to plead guilty to a lesser charge and thus to receive a lighter sentence. But he would have to confess to having stressed the Copernican theory too strongly in his book and with his lectures and letters to audiences and people around Europe. The Church felt that Galileo was moving too fast, and bringing the debate over the Copernican theory into the theological realm instead of just being content to keep the matter as a disputed theory instead of a proven fact.

In his formal abjuration, made on his knees, Galileo was required to say, "I have been judged vehemently suspect of heresy, that is, of having held and believed that the Sun is the center of the universe, and immovable, and that the Earth is not the center of the same, and that it does move. Wishing, however, to remove from the minds of your Eminences and all faithful Christians this vehement suspicion reasonably conceived against me, I abject with a sincere heart and unfeigned faith, I curse and detest the said errors and heresies, and generally all and every error, heresy, and sect contrary to the Holy Catholic Church. And I swear that in the future I will neither say nor assert orally or in writing such things as may bring upon me similar suspicion."

Yet it has passed into popular legend that Galileo muttered (if so, it was fortunately not loud enough to be heard by the tribunal), *"Eppur si muove"*—"And yet it moves."

Accordingly, Galileo was sentenced to prison and to religious penances. He was condemned as "vehemently suspected of heresy" (though three out of 10 cardinals didn't sign the judgment against him). In a formal ceremony, the scientist abjured his "errors," which then allowed him to be under house arrest for the rest of his days. His book was put on the church's "Index of Forbidden Books" as well, where it languished until 1824.

With this measure of freedom he began work on his next opus, *Discourse on Two New Sciences,* which detailed more experiments and provided a guide to scientific methodology.

Though suffering from a hernia in 1634, Galileo was still denied permission to see a doctor in Florence. Furthermore, he was advised that any more such requests could result in re-imprisonment. The Church obviously still considered him a major threat.

Despite his hernia and advancing age, Galileo kept working. In

1636 he sent a proposal to the Dutch government for determining longitude at sea by using eclipses of Jupiter's moons. But the Dutch officials next year opined his theory wouldn't work, though they did decide to give him a valuable gold chain for his efforts. To help restore him to the Church's good graces, Galileo refused to accept the Dutch-given gold chain in 1638, a gesture which led to a commendation by the Pope.

In 1637 Galileo lost the sight in his right eye. In a letter to a friend, he wrote: "The sight in my right eye, that eye whose labors have had such glorious results, is lost forever..." Nevertheless, his research continued, and in the same year—he was now 73—he announced the discovery of a new libration (an oscillatory motion of a heavenly body by which certain parts of it alternately appear and disappear) of the moon. But by the beginning of 1638 the vision in his left eye failed as well, and he became totally blind. Still, his petition to the church to be set free was denied though this time—now that his condition was incurable—he was permitted to go to Florence and be closer to medical help. Curiously, he was also allowed to attend church on religious holidays—but told not to have contact with others.

Aging and blind, and saddened by the death of Virginia, his eldest daughter, Galileo still had the spirit and discipline—and curiosity—to keep working. "Work, and you forget your troubles," he wrote to a friend. He was helped by his son, Vincenzio, who made diagrams and sketches from his father's suggestions.

In 1642, his curiosity undiminished, Galileo died at his Arcetri villa. Even on the day of his death—January 8—he was said to have been busy explaining to his son plans for a new kind of clock that would tell time—minutes and seconds and not just the hours—using a pendulum's swing instead of movement of water or sand.

His last work, *Discoveries Concerning the New Sciences,* was smuggled to Holland and published there in 1638, thus getting around the ongoing Inquisition; but by the time Galileo received a copy of this opus he had lost his sight. While the Church prohibited his works to be published in the Church's political dominions in the Italy of the day, Galileo's writings were studied by scholars throughout the rest of Europe. Invention of the printing press in 1454 had greatly expanded the spread of knowledge in this fashion.

SPLENDID SENIORS

Galileo had wanted to be buried with his ancestors in the basilica of Santa Croce in Florence, but out of fear of Church disapproval, he was buried secretly. The Church did oppose a plan by the Grand Duke of Tuscany to erect a monument for Galileo. But in 1737 a monument was finally put up at the Santa Croce church. And in 1992 the Church—after more than three centuries—admitted it was in error in condemning Galileo.

Some of Galileo's comments:

> *"I do not feel obliged to believe that the same God who has endowed us with sense, reason, and intellect has intended us to forgo their use."*

> *"All truths are easy to understand once they are discovered; the point is to discover them."*

> *"Mathematics is the language with which God has written the universe."*

Isaac Newton
1642–1727

*"I do not know what I may appear to the world, but
to myself I seem to have been only like
a boy playing on the seashore,
and diverting myself in now and then
finding a smoother pebble or a prettier shell
than ordinary, whilst the great ocean of truth
lay all undiscovered before me."*

Despite this modest self-appraisal Isaac Newton became one of the greatest scientists in history, developing theories and methodology that changed the world and became the underpinnings of modern scientific endeavors. But even after his earlier scientific successes, he continued seeking other less scientific truths in religion/theology and alchemy.

The last decades of his long life were consistently active, quite possibly preventing another mental breakdown as he had experienced earlier. He also suffered from gout, among other physical ailments. He kept busy revising his major publications, making studies into ancient history and the role of religion, delving into alchemical research in search of the hidden powers of nature—which some critics found less than scientific—and carrying out his official duties as Warden of the Royal Mint, where his use of informers led him to become the nemesis of counterfeiters in London. Considered to be sensitive to criticism, he faced various challenges to his scientific theories from other scientists and scholars, but continued with his research and subsequent publications. His scientific work has withstood the test of time.

Newton was an ardent biblical scholar, and fluent in ancient languages. One of the tasks he set for himself in his latter years was to reconcile Greek, Jewish and pagan dates and mythology with the Bible. Judeo-Christian prophecies, and their decipherment in relation to an understanding of God, was another of his studies in this field. Basically, Newton argued that the universe could not be as beautiful and orderly as it was without the control levied by some Supreme Being, perhaps foreseeing to some extent the "Intelligent Design" argument of today.

In *The Chronology of Ancient Kingdoms Amended,* which came out in 1728, a year after he died at the age of 85, Newton—already knighted by the Crown—tried to employ astronomical data to put together a chronology of the ancient world, as there was little clear evidence of what had taken place otherwise. This chronology, in turn, would then help illuminate what caused the world's peoples to develop as they had.

None of his research, scientific or otherwise, would have taken place if he had been a better farm manager, an occupation once targeted for him. He was born to a less than affluent farming family in Woolsthorpe, England in the year that Galileo died. Dispatched to Cambridge in 1661 for an alternate career as a preacher, Newton studied mathematics and was much influenced by the teachings of Francis Bacon and René Descartes.

Presence of the plague caused Cambridge to close down, but Newton continued to ponder the world of science as it was known.

In his famous work *Principia,* he formulated four basic and quite revolutionary rules for scientific reasoning: (1) We are to admit no more causes of natural things such as are both true and sufficient to explain their appearance; (2) The same natural effects must be assigned to the same causes; (3) Qualities of bodies are to be esteemed as universal; and (4) Propositions deduced from observation of phenomena should be viewed as accurate until other phenomena contradict them.

In a renowned tale, seeing an apple fall in his orchard around 1665/66 led Newton to deduce that the same natural law of gravitation regulated the motion of the moon as well as the apple. His three laws of motion became the basic principles of modern physics. In *Opticks,* Newton made significant discoveries on the phenomena of light and color. He also developed the mathematical field of calculus.

Honors came to Newton, though he also faced critics and had to overcome a mental breakdown at one point. In response to detractors, he famously said, "If I have seen further, it is by standing on the shoulders of giants."

He was elected a Member of Parliament. He also moved to London to become Warden of the Royal Mint, a position he kept until his death. Elected a fellow of the Royal Society of London in 1671, he became its president in 1703 and was annually reelected for the remainder of his life.

In his later years Newton wrote extensively about religion, with his recondite output generally unpublished, at least during his lifetime. He was raised an Anglican, but his pursuit of metaphysical verities covered the Bible and religious beliefs in general. Among his writings were *Of the Faith which was Once Delivered to the Saints, Paradoxical Questions Concerning the Morals and Actions of Athanasius and his Followers, A Treatise on Revelation,* and *Prophecies of Daniel and the Apocalypse of St. John.*

Newton also wrote extensively on alchemy, which was considered a reasonable field of study in his time. Some suspicions have been raised that his experiments in alchemy may have induced an abiding lead and mercury poisoning. A celibate, he used his eminently rational mind to cope with sexual impulses. "The way to chastity is not to struggle with incontinent thoughts, but to avert the thoughts by some imployment (sic), or by reading, or meditating on other things."

Voltaire, the great French philosopher/writer, penned this comment in *Letters on the English:* "The several discoveries Sir Isaac Newton has made on light are equal to the boldest things which the curiosity of man could expect after so many philosophical novelties."

Newton's mint position gave him financial security, but despite his successes in science, there was a time when he couldn't even pay his dues of one shilling to the Royal Society. The Royal Society fortunately excused him of this obligation. He never married, and lived in a modest fashion. His knighting in 1705 by Queen Anne was said to be the first time that honor had been bestowed on a scientist. He died at 84, disinterested in the Church tending to his final hours. His final honor was being buried in Westminster Abbey, the first scientist to have received that privilege.

Alexander Pope, the famed poet and his contemporary, wrote: "Nature and Nature's laws lay hid in night; God said, Let Newton be, and all was light."

Benjamin Franklin
1706–1790

"Who has deceived you so often as yourself?"

When the battles of Concord and Bunker Hill were fought in 1775, ushering in the Revolutionary War, Benjamin Franklin had reached his 69th year, with a lifetime of illustrious accomplishments already to his credit. Among his many deeds were invention of the lightning rod, the iron furnace stove called the Franklin Stove, bifocal glasses, and a sort of odometer, as well as creation of the first circulating library and his popular annual publication, *Poor Richard's Almanack*, which featured pithy sayings and axioms on traditional values.

But the times were perilous. There was no "nation" as yet that could be said to need him, but certainly his native Philadelphia and the erstwhile "colony" of Pennsylvania did require his counsel; and so did all the people in the 13 colonies who sought a measure first of relief from British rule and ultimately for freedom from England. As one of the "Founding Fathers," Franklin—putting aside the difficulties of his advanced age—spent the rest of his life first creating the nation, then preserving it through the war with England while securing the aid of France as an astute diplomat, and finally helping to steer the fledgling country during its first years.

In May 1775 Franklin was appointed a Pennsylvania delegate to the Second Continental Congress. He was also a member of the Pennsylvania Committee of Safety, as well as a member of a committee for the defense of Philadelphia, which at this time was the largest city in the 13 colonies. He took on the responsibility for the printing of continental currency, for the manufacture of saltpeter, for determining how to provision the army being put together to fight the English, and for organization of the post office. Subsequently, he became the first

Postmaster General.

Despite all his activities, some were suspicious that he was a spy for the English, given his trips to England and associations with leading loyalists. Indeed his own son, William, was a loyalist, which led to a bitter split between them and eventually Franklin disowning William.

Despite his advancing years Franklin was still both innovative and creative, working on the model of a new musket and a boom of logs and iron that could block any movement of English warships on the Delaware River. On the political front, he prepared and read to the Congress a paper in July 1775, "Articles of Confederation and Perpetual Union," which contributed some ideas to the future Constitution yet to come in 1781. Interestingly, he wrote of a "United Colonies" that could conceivably embrace Canada, England's colonies in the West Indies, and even Ireland—if these entities were willing to band together in such a fashion.

When over 70 he participated in a military campaign of nearly a month's duration, with the combatants traveling north to Canada by various boats (not very easy on his body, but he endured the considerable discomfort) and on several waterways in a vain effort to convince the Canadians to join the 13 colonies in their rebellion. The battles against the English didn't go well, however, and the Canadians stayed loyal to the crown. For his efforts, Franklin found his legs swollen with dropsy.

Franklin also became a member of the Committee of Correspondence, which wrote to people around the world to enlist their support of the colonies in their revolt. Not all the letters were exactly standard correspondence, as the group was also active in conducting foreign affairs to some extent, which led to the use of secret codes and other security measures. Obtaining both alliances and arms became primary goals.

He also worked with Thomas Jefferson and others to draft what became the Declaration of Independence. Though the work was primarily attributed to Jefferson, Franklin had a modifying influence on some of the language. At the signing at the end of the Continental Congress, he came out with the famed comment that the signers had "to hang together, or most assuredly we shall all hang separately."

Despite his age, he was selected as one of a commission of three sent to Paris in fall 1776 to negotiate a treaty with France, then England's enemy. This sailing was his seventh venture across the Atlantic Ocean (he made eight overall), and one that enabled him to pursue his interest in the movements of the Gulf Stream. He also devised new watertight bulkheads while mulling over ideas to reduce wind resistance for ships.

In Paris, where he was already well-known and respected, Franklin served his new country well, finally succeeding in lining up the French as allies. He lived well (which led to some criticism), having nine servants at one point and enjoying some sumptuous banquets, which did little for his expanding waistline. Among his sundry activities, he helped pave the way for the nautical heroics of John Paul Jones. In 1779 he even helped plan a joint attack by the Americans and French naval forces against the English coast.

Franklin—who liked to flirt and was eminently capable of *bon mots* as well as flowery letters—was also a favorite in the Parisian salons and of some French ladies. Some memorable quotes were attributed to him during this period, including one to a Madame Helvetius who wanted to know why he was delaying a visit to her. Ever the gallant, Franklin wrote, "Madame, I am waiting until the nights are longer."

Franklin worked sporadically on his *Autobiography of Benjamin Franklin,* an opus he had begun at the age of 65.

In his papers he wrote about various deductions made through the years, such as colds coming from human contact, the dangers of lead poisoning (from handling lead type in printing), and developing—along with Noah Webster—a more phonetic version of English.

Finally, 75 years old and suffering from gout, Franklin sent a letter to Congress from Paris that he was resigning. He also suggested that, given the difficulties of another long sea voyage, he might live out the rest of his days in France. But it was all to no avail, as his resignation was declined—he was just too valuable—and he was named one of five commissioners to handle peace negotiations with England.

Amid all the political activities, Franklin still maintained his keen interest in science. In one letter in 1783 he wrote: "I begin to be almost sorry I was born so soon, since I cannot have the happiness of knowing what will be known 100 years hence."

Finally Congress gave approval for his recall, and he left Paris in

July 1785 for his return trip to Philadelphia. But his public service was far from over as, at the age of 79, he was selected as president of the Supreme Executive Council of Pennsylvania, a role he kept for three years. And, as a spokesman for the new country, he published a pamphlet, *Information to Those Who Would Remove to America,* that encouraged selective immigration and extolled the virtues of the new country. Ahead of the times, he also became president in 1787 of the Pennsylvania Society for Promoting the Abolition of Slavery.

At the Constitutional Convention of 1787, when the constitution of the U.S. was hammered out, he was a force for compromise between competing factions. Showing great prescience, he sought for ways to keep money out of the political process. "There are two passions," he contended, "which have a powerful influence on the affairs of men. These are ambition and avarice: the love of power, and the love of money. Separately, each of these has great force in prompting men to action, but when united in view of the same object, they have in many minds the most violent of effects."

In his closing address, referring to changes in his opinions on various subjects (including his now disapproving of slavery), he said: " . . . the older I grow, the more apt I am to doubt my own judgment and pay more respect to the judgment of others."

Asked for his opinion of the Convention's results, he famously replied, "A republic, if you can keep it."

Living with his daughter in Philadelphia, Franklin contended with his declining health with his customary common sense. He wrote to a friend: "As I live temperately, drink no wine, and use daily the exercise of the dumbbell, I flatter myself that the (kidney) stone is kept from augmenting so much as it might otherwise do, and that I may still continue to find it tolerable. People who live long, who will drink the cup of life to the very bottom, must expect to meet with some of the usual dregs."

Franklin still found time to work on some new inventions: a rocking chair that could fan you at the same time you were rocking, a long arm-like object with a claw at the end that could move books placed on high shelves (which he could no longer easily reach), and a footstool that could double as a ladder. He finally left public service only in 1788, when he was 82. Even when bedridden he held meetings of the American Philosophical Society in his home. Death came in 1790. Many mourners attended his funeral.

Among his many quotes: An outline giving reasons for men to choose older women in their love life ended: "Lastly, they are so grateful."

"By failing to plan, you are planning to fail."

"Diligence is the mother of good luck."

"At 20 years of age the will reigns; at 30 the wit; at 40 the judgment."

"Admiration is the daughter of ignorance."

"Half the truth is often a great lie."

"If a man could have half his wishes, he would double his troubles."

"Any fool can criticize, condemn and complain, and most fools do."

"Keep your eyes wide open before marriage, half shut afterwards."

"To find out a girl's faults, praise her to her girlfriends."

"Many men die at 25 and aren't buried until they're 75."

"Those that beat swords into plowshares usually end up plowing for those who don't."

Benjamin Disraeli
1804–1881

"There are three kinds of lies:
lies, damn lies, and statistics."

Benjamin Disraeli, the famed 19th century English prime minister and author, was also considered one of the great wits of his age.

Some of his greatest accomplishments came after he was 65 and suffering from gout, asthma, and fading eyesight, among other ailments. Dentures for poor teeth presented another discomfort, especially during speeches. At one speech he had the dexterity to quickly reinsert his dentures, which had plopped out, by turning around as if to ask someone a question and thus avoiding attention.

During his first stint as prime minister, which began in 1866, he helped gain passage of the 1867 Reform Act, which gave the vote to many more men. After being voted out of power in 1868, he returned as prime minister in 1874, when he was 70. In power again, he commented, "I am in the sunset of life, but I do not despair of seeing my purpose effected."

Nonetheless, Disraeli saw to passage several major domestic reforms covering health, pure foods and drugs, education, and factory working conditions as the industrial age was settling in. On the international front his policies were expansionist, and he was to a large extent responsible for England gaining possession of the Suez Canal. His famed comment to Queen Victoria was, "It is just settled; you have it, Madam."

In 1876 he had Queen Victoria, with whom he enjoyed a strong relationship, named the Empress of India. Disraeli was helpful in drawing the queen out of her prolonged mourning over the death of her husband, Prince Consort Albert. He also successfully mediated a resolution to the Russo-Turkish War of 1878–79 at the Congress of Berlin in 1878 when he was a weary 73, thus maintaining a balance of power and avoiding more carnage in the Balkans. Disraeli sparred successfully with Bismarck, the leading German statesman, who later commented in admiration, *"Der alte Jude, das ist der Mann!"*—'The Old Jew, that is the Man!"

Disraeli also managed to obtain Cyprus for the British Empire. On the political front, he created the Conservative General Office, which some political scientists rate as the antecedent of modern political party organizations.

In 1876 he was made the first Lord Beaconsfield by a grateful queen. Thereafter, he sat in the House of Lords and not in the more powerful House of Commons. He retired in 1880, when his great political rival, William Gladstone, became prime minister. With more time he returned to writing novels, and was working on an untitled opus until his death in 1881. He kept corresponding with Queen Victoria with some 22 letters, marked by more personal matters than politics.

Disraeli was born in London to an Italian Sephardic Jewish family. When he was 13 his father had his entire family baptized. Not being Jewish any more greatly impacted his political career, though many people still considered him to be a Jew. It wasn't until 1858 that Jews were allowed to become members of Parliament.

Disraeli pursued both literary and political careers, and was much more successful at the former. He is often credited with creating the political novel, and his works often had thinly disguised characters from among his contemporaries. Among his novels, many with a political background, were *Vivian Grey* (which came out in 1826 when he was a mere 22), *Lothair, Sybil, The Young Duke, Contarini Fleming, Henrietta Temple,* and *Tancred.* Fighting off occasional bouts of depression, he finished *Endymion* in 1880, a novel he had begun several years earlier.

His first four attempts to be voted into Parliament ended in failure, though he was noted as an effective speaker—as well as a dandy due to his dress. In 1838 he was finally successful. However, his maiden speech in Parliament was a disaster, with other members shouting at him. Undeterred, he uttered the prophetic words "…though I sit down now, the time will come when you will hear me."

After stints as Chancellor of the Exchequer, he finally became prime minister in 1868 and quipped: "Yes, I have climbed to the top of the greasy pole."

Sometimes considered to be England's first and only Jewish prime minister, Disraeli was in fact a practicing Anglican. Disraeli was also unusual in that he rose from the middle class to this pinnacle of power, unlike his predecessors as prime minister, who came from more aristocratic circles. While he didn't identify himself as Jewish, he was castigated and condemned by many with no shortage of anti-Semitic canards.

Disraeli died in 1881 and had a private funeral at his request. Many luminaries came. Flags were flown at half mast, and peals sounded at many cathedrals.

Among the many famous quotes Disraeli made, several related to his ongoing disputes with Gladstone.

At one social event, Gladstone said, "I predict, sir, that you will be die either by hanging or of some vile disease." Disraeli's rejoinder was quick and sharp: "That all depends, sir, upon whether I embrace your policies or your mistress."

Another sally at his favorite target: "William Gladstone has not a single redeeming defect."

And: "If Gladstone fell into the Thames (River), that would be a misfortune; if anybody pulled him out, that I suppose would be a calamity."

On dealing with royalty, he said, "You have heard me called a flatterer, and it is true. Everyone likes flattery; and when you come to royalty, you should lay it on with a trowel."

In once advising a cleric about a sermon where the queen would be present, he said, "If you preach 30 minutes, Her Majesty will be bored. If you preach 15 minutes, Her Majesty will be pleased. If you preach 10 minutes, Her Majesty will be delighted." Yet, from various accounts, he really liked Queen Victoria, with the feeling mutual.

As a personal motto, he chose "Nothing is difficult to the strong."

On some other subjects:

"There is no gambling like politics."

"Finality is not the language of politics."

"Something unpleasant is coming when men are anxious to tell the truth."

"Where knowledge ends, religion begins."

"The disappointment of manhood succeeds the delusion of youth."

"I never deny; I never contradict; I sometimes forget."

"It destroys one's nerves to be amiable every day to the same human being."

"Books are companions even if you don't open them."

"A precedent embalms a principle."

"Grief is the agony of an instant; the indulgence of grief the blunder of a life."

"It is much easier to be critical than correct."

"Like all great travelers, I have seen more than I remember, and remember more than I have seen."

"The fool wonders, the wise man asks."

"Youth is a blunder, manhood a struggle, and old age a regret."

Yet Disraeli's legacy gave mankind and his country much to remember and applaud.

Louis Pasteur
1822–1895

"Chance favors only the prepared mind."

This belief dominated the mind and work of Louis Pasteur, a French chemist and biologist who was one of the greatest humanitarians in the history of the world. His discoveries have formed a cornerstone of many branches of modern medicine—including microbiology, virology, immunology, molecular biology, and stereochemistry—and have saved countless lives. He also helped create a clearer link between theory and practice as it applies to science and the medical field.

Pasteur continued his work despite health problems, including a cerebral hemorrhage he suffered in 1868 that left parts of his left arm and leg incapacitated.

The Pasteur Institute was founded in 1886, when he was 66, as a clinic, research center, and teaching facility. Pasteur devoted the last seven years of his life, though in declining health (at one point his wife read newspapers to him to conserve his eyesight), to continue his efforts and to train new scientists. Disciples were taught two key rules of modern research: Be creative and use your imagination, but apply thorough experimentation for any theory.

"Do not put forward anything that you cannot prove by experimentation," he said. "Imagination should give wings to our thoughts, but we always need decisive experimental proof; and when the moment comes to draw conclusions and to interpret the gathered observations, imagination must be checked and documented by the factual results of the experiment."

Other Pasteur Institutes have been founded around the world. The first foreign one was in 1891 in Saigon (Ho Chi Minh City today) in Vietnam. The latest was the Pasteur Institute of Shanghai, inaugurated in October 2004. Eight scientists trained at the Pasteur Institute have received Nobel Prizes in science.

In reference to these sites, Pasteur wrote, "I beseech you to take interest in these sacred domains so expressively called laboratories. Ask that there be more and that they be adorned, for these are the temples of the future, wealth, and well-being. It is here that humanity will grow, strengthen and improve. Here, humanity will learn to read progress and individual harmony in the works of nature, while humanity's own works are all too often those of barbarism, fanaticism and destruction."

Pasteur, a strong advocate of applied science (not just concentrating on theoretical studies but seeking practical solutions) is most famous for his advocacy of how germs cause infectious diseases, and the development of the technique of vaccines and preventive inoculation. His stress on the importance of antiseptic methods for doctors had a tremendous impact on the treatment of patients. On the personal side, his authoritarian stance and stiff approach in his work and findings didn't always go over well with others.

Pasteur also developed a technique for destroying microorganisms in beverages, under the belief that one way people became afflicted with germs came through their intake of food and beverages. "Pasteurization," which entered the English vocabulary, has since nearly eradicated contaminated milk as a source of infection by germs. Pasteur also developed a technique for inoculating people with a vaccine against rabies, then almost always an incurable disease, and to vaccinate dogs against being affected with rabies. Another achievement was development of an anthrax vaccine.

Application of his basic theories and methods have helped other scientists develop vaccines for typhus and polio. He kept copious handwritten notes in over 100 notebooks, though suspicions were raised that he edited some of his experiments to suggest more success with his theories and experiments.

Pasteur was born in Dole, France and went to college in Paris. He received his doctorate in crystallography in 1847. At the age of 26 he became renowned for his research on molecular asymmetry, with his work becoming the basis for the new science of stereochemistry, a branch of chemistry that deals with the spatial arrangement of atoms and groups in molecules.

He served on the faculty of science at Dijon and then taught at Strasbourg University, where he met his wife, Marie. Supposedly he was so wrapped up in his lab work he had to be reminded to go to church for his wedding. His bride must have forgiven such behavior, if true, as they were married for 46 years. While his wife did occasionally upbraid him as a workaholic, Pasteur commented to a friend, "I console her by telling her I will lead her to posterity."

In 1854 he was appointed Dean and Professor of Chemistry at the faculty of sciences at Lille. During this period Emperor Napoleon III asked Pasteur to investigate diseases affecting the French wine industry. Pasteur then managed to prove that the diseases spoiling wine came from microorganisms that could be destroyed by heating the wine. Pasteur reasoned that if germs caused fermentation, they could also cause diseases in other beverages. Extending this breakthrough to milk led to "pasteurization," which destroys dangerous microbes by heat without also destroying the food. This method is widely used now throughout the world.

Unafraid to challenge prevalent theories, Pasteur disproved the theory of "spontaneous generation," a belief held for centuries that life could emerge spontaneously from non-living matter. He established that specific microorganisms caused specific kinds of fermentation, and the existence of life without oxygen. "Fermentation," he wrote, "is the consequence of life without air. There is no circumstance known in which it can be affirmed that microscopic beings come into the world without germs, without parents similar to themselves."

His discovery of anaerobic life also led to the study of germ-caused diseases like gangrene and septicemia. However, as late as 1875 some doctors were loath to admit that important diseases could be caused by germs. Pasteur became active in advocating significant changes in hospital practices and procedures to lessen the spread of disease by germs. In a talk before the Academy of Medicine in Paris Pasteur argued, "This water, this sponge, this lint with which you wash or cover a wound, may deposit germs which have the power of multiplying rapidly within the tissue. If I had the honor of being a surgeon, not only would I use none but perfectly clean instruments, but I would clean my hands with the greatest care."

In 1876, Pasteur tried to carve out a political career with a race for the Senate, but he came in last in the vote.

Pasteur died in 1895 near Paris. His remains are in a crypt at the Pasteur Institute in Paris. He was buried as a national hero, with thousands attending his funeral.

His sayings include:

"The objective of scientific research is the improvement of human health."

"There are no such things as applied sciences, only applications of science."

"Science knows no country, because knowledge belongs to humanity, and is the torch which illuminates the world."

Susan B. Anthony
1820–1906

"The older I get, the greater power
I seem to have to help the world;
I am like a snowball—the further I am rolled
the more I gain."

Throughout a long life Susan Anthony fought tirelessly for women's rights, especially the right to vote. Her efforts culminated in the 19th Amendment to the U.S. Constitution, though she didn't live to see it become a reality.

She also strived to gain for women such other improvements in their status as the right for equal pay with men, the right to control their own property, and the right to keep their children in case of divorce. A pioneer in the first feminist movement in the U.S., Anthony kept active well after her 65th birthday, despite being slowed down somewhat by advancing age. She organized the International Woman Suffrage Alliance in 1904, when she was past her 80th year.

Overall, Anthony believed that social progress in the U.S. couldn't happen unless women were granted equal rights.

She was born on Feb. 15, 1820 in Adams, Massachusetts. Her father, who dominated family life, was a Quaker abolitionist, a cotton manufacturer, and a stern man who fostered sound principles, self-discipline, and strong convictions. Unfortunately, he felt that many childhood diversions worked against installation of these values, which led to a fine education but a less than carefree childhood. Nonetheless, quite precocious, Anthony learned to read and write at the tender age of three.

The family moved in 1826 to Battensville in upstate New York. Anthony began teaching at a Quaker academy for women, as teaching was about the only profession available for women. Her first involvement with a movement affecting women was the campaign for temperance, which was intended to limit the abuses inflicted to women and children by alcoholic husbands and fathers. Independent-minded, she gave her first public speech for the Daughters of Temperance, and then helped found the Women's State Temperance Society of New York, which was one of the first feminist organizations created in the U.S. However, she felt that women were limited in the scope of their efforts.

From around 1852 to the end of her life she continued to argue, promote and petition for more women's rights. Her efforts even included wearing the famed "bloomer" of the period, a shirt and loose trousers as a sartorial symbol of protest against the more restrictive garments worn by women. Following her father's footprints, she supported the anti-slavery movement from 1856 to the outbreak of the Civil War, and served as an agent for the Anti-Slavery Association. She also participated in the Daughters of Temperance to lessen the substantial amount of male drunkenness that impacted wives and families.

In 1851 she met Elizabeth Cady Stanton, another staunch advocate of women's rights, who had orchestrated the seminal 1848 meeting in Seneca Falls in upstate New York. A declaration of women's rights emerged at this meeting, and another one in Rochester three years later, calling for suffrage, for women to be paid as much as men for the same work, for women to be able to own property, etc. The two women bonded and worked together afterwards.

Unlike Stanton, Anthony never married despite some proposals. She said remaining single allowed her to dedicate herself to the cause of women's rights. "I would not object to marriage if it were not that women throw away every plan, and purpose of their life, to conform to the plans and purposes of the man's life." In a related comment, she declared, "I look for the day when the woman who has a political or judicial brain will have as much right to sit on the Supreme Bench (Court) or in the Senate as men have now. And this time will come."

The pair helped to publish *The Revolution,* a New York-based liberal weekly, in 1868–70, editorializing for equal pay for women with men. Anthony also helped organize the New York Working Women's Association.

A major protest arose in 1872 when Anthony demanded that women be given the same civil and political rights as black males received in the 14th and 15th Amendments. She led a group of women to the election booths in Rochester as a test of the right of women to vote. Arrested, she still managed afterwards to conduct lecture tours that brought a large measure of publicity to her cause. The fees for lectures also enabled her to support herself as a single woman. Undaunted, in March 1873 she again tried to vote in municipal elections. Finally tried and convicted of violating the election laws, she avoided paying the $100 fine levied by arguing the laws were unconstitutional. Her argument, given in a speech, centered on the point that the basic rights of Americans were for "we, the people, not we, the white male citizens."

Anthony kept chipping away at male preserves. While some in the movement were satisfied by the actions of some states in grudgingly giving women more rights, Anthony held out for an amendment to the Constitution. She was tireless in her efforts, even beyond her 65th birthday, and extremely effective in her lectures and writings in rousing sentiment and supporters as well as in organizing the myriad details of the overall movement. Many elected officials were surprised by the number of letters and other material they received from their constituents as a result of Anthony's work.

She spent a great deal of time traveling, well past the age of 65. She allocated a good deal of time for the emerging western territories and states, which necessitated quite a few rough stagecoach rides to reach isolated areas not yet connected by rail.

At the 1860 woman's rights convention Anthony broached the subject of improving the rights of women under current divorce laws. This measure generated considerable opposition from both men and women who felt marriage should be for life. One man, an abolitionist who did favor more women's rights, but not when divorce was the subject, told her, "You are not married. You have no business to be discussing marriage."

Sharp-witted and not at a loss for a comeback, Anthony replied, "Well, you are not a slave. Suppose you quit lecturing on slavery."

The Civil War put a brake on the women's rights movement. After the conflict, Anthony and cohorts sought to have the new 14th Amendment enlarged to cover women's rights. However, despite her move to Washington D.C. to lobby for this and other measures, Congress—clearly male-dominated—wasn't ready for major changes in this area. However, more states passed women's rights legislation during the latter part of the 19th century. Ultimately, after her death, the 19th Amendment (sometimes referred to as the Susan B. Anthony Amendment), gave women the vote in 1920.

Anthony helped compile and publish the massive four volume *History of Woman Suffrage* during 1881–1902, and in 1888—when she was already 68—she helped organize the International Council of Women. She became president of the National American Woman Suffrage Association and held the position until 1900. One of her parting comments in a speech in Washington D.C. was "Failure is impossible!" (Bringing to mind the latter-day space exploration axiom, "Failure is not an option.") She was right.

Acclaimed worldwide for her work, Anthony died at Rochester, N.Y. on March 13, 1906.

The U.S. issued a silver dollar bearing her image in 1979, the first coin to depict a woman in U.S. history. The Susan B. Anthony House in Rochester, where she lived, is now a national landmark and museum.

Among her quotes:

"Independence is happiness."

"Men, their rights and nothing more; women, their rights and nothing less."

"I always distrust people who know so much about what God wants them to do to their fellows."

"The religious persecution of the ages has been done under what was claimed to be the command of God."

"There will never be complete equality until women themselves help to make laws and elect lawmakers."

"Cautious, careful people, always casting about to preserve their reputation and social status, never can bring about a reform."

Henrik Ibsen
1828–1906

"Never wear your best trousers
when you go out to fight for freedom and truth."

One of the greatest and most influential dramatists of the 19th century, the Norwegian playwright Henrik Ibsen wrote some of his most acclaimed works while living away from his native country. But in the process he put Norway, which received its independence from Denmark during the earlier part of his life, on the map of Europe and the world. Only Shakespeare has had more of his plays produced around the world than Ibsen.

Many young playwrights have studied Ibsen's themes and techniques, which centered on revealing the facades and hypocrisy behind bourgeois society, the gap middle-class people experienced between their desires and their everyday lives, and their need to be truthful to themselves in facing traditional, comfortable, but out-of-date conventions. The conflicts in facing facts, a prime requirement to living an honest life, dominated his latter works. His plays challenging the existing order and revealing profound insights into people's lives generated bitter opposition from conservative quarters in Norway, and other countries as well. His acuity in dramatizing his psychological observations led some to dub him the "Freud of the theater."

Ibsen, who was usually a rebel of sorts against the entrenched community, also argued that the majority in society tended to settle for the status quo and to resist change on key subjects like politics and religion.

Ibsen published his last drama, *When We Dead Awaken,* in 1899 when he was 71. Other plays written in the early 1890s, when he was already in his senior years, were *The Master Builder* and *John Gabriel Borkman.*

Ibsen was born in the coastal village of Skien in 1828. He left school at 15 to become an assistant to a pharmacist in Grimstad, where he fathered an illegitimate son and then was forced to pay paternity costs for 14 years. He wanted to become a doctor, but failed a university entrance test. Involvement with a revolutionary movement—Europe was still recoiling from the series of uprisings in 1848—soured him on political efforts. The world of theater drew him, and he spent a considerable number of years involved in different aspects of the stage.

At the newly established National Theatre in Bergen he became the "writer in residence" when he was only 23. Influenced by the historical plays of Shakespeare, he wrote four romantic historical plays during this period. *The Burial Mound* was produced in 1850. *The Pretenders* appeared in 1863.

In 1857 he went to Christiana (which is now Oslo), Norway's capital, to become artistic director of the new Norwegian Theater. He also got married. When the theater sank into bankruptcy in the 1860s he finally petitioned the government for a writing grant, which was not extended. However, the government did supply a small writer's stipend to let him travel to other parts of Europe starting in 1864, when he was 36. In a substantial exile of sorts he lived abroad in Rome, Berlin and Dresden for the next 27 years.

In 1866, while living in Italy, he wrote a verse drama, *Brand,* which was sold in book form and not originally intended to be produced on stage. *Brand* became so successful that the Norwegian government gave him a small pension for life. *Peer Gynt,* which he wrote in 1867, further cemented his reputation as one of the leading dramatists in Europe. The government even selected Ibsen to represent the country at the opening of the Suez Canal in 1869.

After a period of writing prose dramas, he concentrated in the next couple of decades on writing more naturalistic and realistic plays using everyday language. Some of his most notable and most produced plays ensued, including *Pillars of Society* and *A Doll's House* in 1877, *Ghosts* in 1881, *An Enemy of the People* in 1882, *The Wild Duck* in 1884, and *Hedda Gabler* in 1890. Ibsen considered his 1873 play, *Emperor and Galilean,* to be his finest work, but the judgment of history accords much higher status to his other major plays.

Ghosts, in particular, caused an uproar by scandalizing audiences with its frank dramatization of the impact of "the sins of the fathers" and hereditary syphilis—though the theme was much broader, with the title also referring to outdated beliefs. The subject matter helped usher in more realistic dramas. The play was turned down by Scandinavian theaters, with its premiere performance at a Chicago theater in 1882. Ibsen was hardly surprised, commenting, *"Ghosts* will probably cause alarm in certain circles, but that cannot be helped. If it did not, it would not have been necessary to write it."

Ibsen was also a poet, and had a collection of his poems published in 1871.

Ibsen returned to Oslo as a national hero in 1891. He received homage as one of the world's great writers in 1898, on his 70th birthday. He continued writing until he had a stroke at the turn of the century that left him incapacitated until his death in 1906 at the age of 78. He was honored with a state funeral. A Centre for Ibsen Studies continues the study of his plays.

Some of Ibsen's comments:

> *"Life would be all right if we didn't have to put up with these damned creditors who keep pestering us with the demands of their ideals."*

> *"My main goal has been to depict people, human moods and human fates, on the basis of certain predominant social conditions and perceptions."*

> *"The great secret of power is never to will to do more than you can accomplish."*

> *"The strongest man of the world is he who stands alone."*

> *"Castles in the air—they are so easy to take refuge in. And so easy to build, too."*

> *"It is not the conscious strife between ideas parading before us; nor is this the situation in real life. What we see are human conflicts, and enwrapped in these, deep inside, lay ideas at battle— being defeated, or charged with victory."*

*"It is inexcusable for scientists to torture animals;
let them make their experiments on journalists and politicians."*

*"The majority is never right. Never, I tell you.
That's one of these lies in society that no free and intelligent man
can help rebelling against. Who are the people
that make up the biggest proportion of the population—
the intelligent ones or the fools?"*

Leo Tolstoy
1828–1910

"The one thing that is necessary,
in life as in art,
is to tell the truth."

Despite any pain to himself, to others in his family, and to his country of Russia as well, Tolstoy lived up to this credo in his many writings. His bouts with venereal disease and gambling debts were all examined. While excommunicated by the Russian Orthodox Church in 1901 for his social/religious views, his philosophy of nonviolent resistance to evil (state-sponsored and otherwise) greatly influenced both Mahatma Gandhi in India and Nelson Mandela in South Africa.

In 1902 Tolstoy warned the Tsar that civil war would develop unless more freedom was given to the Russian people. More unrest occurred in Russia until civil war did break out less than two decades later.

Tolstoy continued writing and advocating his beliefs, including the importance of the individual conscience in opposition to collective morality, well past his 65th birthday. Mankind, he argued, was naturally good, with civilization a corrupting influence. The important life of man only started when his spiritual element overcame his animal impulses.

One early comment in his diary: "The man whose only goal is own happiness is bad; he whose goal is the good opinion of others is weak; he whose goal is the happiness of others is good; he whose goal is God is great!" Not living up to these points throughout his life led to much mental wringing on his part.

Writing until close to his last days, Tolstoy even rode his first bicycle at the age of 67, and continuing riding until he was already 80, gaining the admiration of children and the surprise of some adults. Lifting dumbbells and riding horseback were other exercises taken in his senior years.

His major works *War and Peace* and *Anna Karenina* were written earlier in his life. But many significant works were produced after he was 65. *Resurrection,* a novel that came out in 1899, when he was 71, was his last major work. Lesser known was a novella, *Hadji Murad,* penned in 1904 but not published until 1912, two years after his death. This work, detailing his experiences in the Russian wars against the Chechens and other groups in the Caucasus in the mid 19th century, prefigured to a considerable extent the current conflict in that volatile area. *Twenty-Three Tales* came out in 1905.

The Kingdom of God Is Within You, the heart of his beliefs, emerged spottily in 1893 after several years of work. While prohibited by the censors, typed copies made their way across Russia. Translations that sprang up abroad heightened his reputation and inspired many with his simple but strong message. "What Is Art?," a censored essay in 1898, also drew the wrath of some artists who disputed Tolstoy's calling for art to reflect morality.

When introduced to the new medium of cinema, Tolstoy even considered that he might write a screenplay in the future. With substantial foresight he envisioned that "with this technique one could reach huge masses of people, all the peoples of the Earth!"

In his writings Tolstoy displayed a tremendous insight into human nature, along with a distinctive ability to reveal character. Deep philosophical values were carefully woven into memorable descriptions of historical events. In some instances, ordinary and everyday occurrences were described with telling perception. A considerable amount of his output stemmed from his richly detailed journals, which covered his problems of gambling and syphilis.

His estate at Yasnaya Polyana ("clear glade") was visited by hundreds of people eager to see the white-bearded author. In his later years he tried to show more allegiance to the peasantry. Some said this led to his paying less attention to his own personal appearance. Believing education was the main way to solve society's ills, he opened a school for peasants at his estate. To see the real world and its miseries he once went on a pilgrimage dressed as a peasant (with two disguised bodyguards not far off) to the Optima-Pustyn Monastery. His activities brought police surveillance, with the State suspicious of his agitating peasants (the serfs had been freed in 1861 by the Tsar) with notions of equality. His essays such as "What Then Must We Do?" were censored; works that went through were edited.

The Church was similarly unhappy with his arguments that it had misused the teachings of Christ, and eventually he was excommunicated.

Tolstoy, though wealthy himself, held a dim view of some peers. He said, "I cannot rejoice at the birth of a child into the wealthy class; it is the proliferation of parasites."

When he didn't get the Nobel Prize for literature in 1902, which many felt he deserved, Tolstoy merely said, "I was very pleased to learn that the Nobel Prize was not given to me. First, because it spared me the great problem of disposing of the money, which, like all money, can only lead to evil, in my view…"

Tolstoy also tried to extricate himself from the responsibility of possessions. In 1908 he wrote a will surrendering all his copyrights. (A new will was later presented behind his back changing his desire.) In 1910, eager to live his last years as a wandering ascetic (with his doctor in tow), he left home. He didn't get far. He fell ill at the rail station at the small town of Astapovo and died a few days later of pneumonia at the age of 82. The Church tried unsuccessfully to get a death-bed return to the faith (no religious services were permitted), while the police prepared for riots.

Some of his quotes:

*"Everyone thinks of changing the world,
but no one thinks of changing himself."*

"The two most powerful warriors are patience and time."

*"What counts in a happy marriage
is not so much how compatible you are,
but how you deal with incompatibility."*

Mark Twain
1835–1910

*"**Life** would be infinitely happier if we could only be born
at the age of 80 and gradually approach 18."*

Samuel Langhorne Clemens, probably the best and most famous
humorist in American history, grew up in Hannibal, Missouri, a
Mississippi River town. He became a river pilot, which led later to his
pseudonym of "Mark Twain," the river cry to indicate a two-fathom
water depth. He used this pseudonym, chosen when he was a young
journalist in San Francisco, for close to 50 years.

In 1900, when he turned 65, he came out with *The Man Who
Corrupted Hadleyburg & Other Stories & Essays* and "English As She Is
Taught."Among his other post-65 works are *A Double-Barrelled Detec-
tive Story,* 1902; *My Debut as a Literary Person & Other Essays & Stories,*
1903; "A Dog's Tale" and "Extracts from Adam's Diary," 1904; "What
Is Man?" and *The $30,000 Bequest & Other Stories,* 1906; *Christian Sci-
ence* and "A Horse's Tale," 1907; and "Is Shakespeare Dead? From My
Autobiography" and "Extract from Captain Stormfield's Visit to Heav-
en," 1909. His *The Mysterious Stranger* was published posthumously
in 1916.

But Twain is best known for earlier works.

His career began when he went west to seek his fortune and
eventually turned to journalism, both in Virginia City, Nevada during
the silver furor (he had no luck in his prospecting) and then San
Francisco. In San Francisco he began to develop his distinctive style
of humor writing for local publications, first using his pseudonym in
1863. One example was his take on weather in the Bay City. "It has only
snowed twice in San Francisco in 19 years and then it only remained on
the ground long enough to astonish the children." A camping outing at
Lake Tahoe led to this comment, "The air up there in the clouds is very

pure and fine, bracing and delicious. And why shouldn't it be? It is the same the angels breathe."

Fame came to him with publication of "The Celebrated Jumping Frog of Calaveras County" in 1865. Books came in succession, including *The Innocents Abroad* in 1869, *Roughing It* in 1870, *Adventures of Tom Sawyer* in 1876, and perhaps his most celebrated book, *The Adventures of Huckleberry Finn,* in 1884.

Huckleberry Finn has been marked by many critics as the first truly American novel. Many prior American novels used more formal English, with Twain's novel incorporating a distinctive American version of the English language. *Huckleberry Finn* has been translated into more than 50 languages and is part of many academic curriculums. It isn't very controversial today, but its language about black people led some observers in previous decades to accuse Twain of racism, while others considered his language to be truly reflective of the American scene in the period he wrote about. His use of a boy to relate the story in first person, and using the vernacular, were literary innovations.

Giving lectures to the tune of $100–$150 a talk became another activity. His first professional lecture was given in San Francisco in 1866, when he was 30. He developed a strong sense of timing and delivery that he used throughout his life, which included hundreds of lectures and speeches.

Twain married and lived a more sedate life in Hartford, Connecticut and the Quarry Farm near Elmira, N.Y., while continuing to write. However, financial investments—especially in new kinds of printing machines—didn't pan out, and he fell into debt. He invested around $50,000 in a "kaolatype," a new way to print illustrations, and even more—$300,000—for the "Paige Compositor," a sort of robotic machine to replace typesetting by a person. To make money to pay his debts he went on a lecture tour around the world. *Following the Equator* came out in 1897.

His personality, and his work, turned more serious in his later years, especially with the deaths of two of his daughters in 1896 and 1909, and his wife, Livy, in 1904 when he was 69. His opinion was often sought on important public issues. He felt, for example, that reparations were due to black Americans. While unopposed to the growth of Christian Science, he did satirize the faith's founder, Mary Baker

Eddy, as a "shameless old swindler."

In his latter years he also took to often wearing white suits, with this attire becoming sort of a sartorial trademark. One suggestion was that he preferred white to offset depressing elements of his life, and that dark clothing came too close to his occasional mindset. However, he may have just reasoned that wearing white made him stand out while also giving a more hygienic appearance. Regardless of his mood, however, he never lost his capacity for satirical and witty comments. When media reports mistakenly announced that he had died, Twain said, "Reports of my death have been greatly exaggerated."

A signal honor came in 1907 when Oxford University in England awarded him an honorary doctorate of laws degree. He was even given a garden party by King Edward VII.

Seeking the infusion of youth into his life, absent the presence of grandchildren, Twain befriended some mothers and their daughters, whom he met while traveling. Correspondence led to creation of a small group in 1808 that he dubbed the "Aquarium Club" while calling the young girl members "Angelfish."

Twain died on April 21, 1910. Many public tributes were given throughout the country. A monument, two fathoms high, marks his burial site in Elmira, N.Y.

Among his many notable witticisms:

*"Reader, suppose you were an idiot.
And suppose you were a member of Congress.
But I repeat myself."*

*"I believe that our Heavenly Father invented man
because he was disappointed in the monkey."*

*"It is curious—curious that physical courage should be so common
in the world, and moral courage so rare."*

*"Ah, well, I am a great and sublime fool. But then I am God's fool,
and all His works must be contemplated with respect."*

*"What is the chief end of man? To get rich.
In what way—dishonestly if we can; honestly, if we must."*

*"Get your facts first, and then you can distort them
as much as you please."*

*"If you pick up a starving dog and make him prosperous,
he will not bite you. This is the principal difference
between a dog and a man."*

"Nothing needs reforming as other people's habits."

*"It's not what we don't know that hurts us;
rather, what gets us into trouble
is what we are absolutely certain of
that just ain't so."*

*"Let us endeavor to live that when we come to die
even the undertaker will be sorry."*

Mary Baker Eddy
1821–1910

"When the heart speaks, however simple the words,
its language is always acceptable to those who have hearts."

Mary Baker Eddy founded a religion, Christian Science, as well as one of the most respected newspapers in the U.S., *The Christian Science Monitor,* among her many achievements. At the start of the 20th century, when she was well over 65, she was widely considered to be one of the most influential women in the country.

As the new faith grew in adherents, she also continued writing treatises. In 1898 she created a publishing company including a weekly magazine. At the age of 86, in 1908, she founded *The Christian Science Monitor* to overcome the "yellow journalism" of tabloids of the day (which had, to some extent, been directed at her). The newspaper, whose motto is "to injure no man, but to bless all mankind," has since gone on to win several Pulitzer Prizes.

But Eddy had to face considerable criticism, which included claims of plagiarism, mesmerism, over-commercialization of her teachings/church and excessive claims of success. Disapproval and doubt about the efficacy of her message of mental healing, along with the religious connotations, also made her church and herself suspect in some circles. Her identification of herself as a "Professor of Obstetrics" in advertising notices in *The Christian Science Journal* generated no shortage of adverse comments. She was satirized by Mark Twain (who termed her a "shameless old swindler") and faced less-than-accurate newspaper articles; vying newspaper chains fought for which could put out more lurid stories painting her as dead, near dead, or incapacitated to the point of being handled by a cabal. One accusation held that an impersonator was in place. She finally overcame a bitter "Next Friends" court case around 1908 that had alleged she was mentally incompetent.

The suing parties withdrew their suit with clear-cut evidence through interviews that she was well even if reclusive.

In one denial of various charges, made in 1885, she wrote, "That I take opium, that I am an infidel, a mesmerist, a medium, a pantheist, or that my hourly life is prayerless, or not in strict obedience to the Mosaic Decalogue, is not more true than that I am dead, as is oft reported."

Despite the criticism, the new church continued to grow, and by 1900 there were branches in most major U.S. cities. She was increasingly asked to comment on topical issues of the day by media.

Eddy was born and raised near Concord, New Hampshire in a relatively strict Calvinist ethos. For the most part she was educated at home. Her first marriage ended while she was pregnant. A son was born later. Consistently in poor health, she decided to experiment with alternative healing methods including homeopathy, mesmerism and hydropathy. She came under the influence of a Doctor Phineas Quimby, a mental healer in Portland, Maine who advocated a medicine-free system he called "The Science of Health and Happiness." The extent to which his ideas were incorporated into her theories became a controversial issue in later years, with some charging her with theft of his philosophy of healing and failing to credit him as being the real founder of the faith, at least in providing the genesis. But Eddy is certainly credited with being the founder of the formal faith of Christian Science and of having the spiritual and organizational strength and leadership to develop this religion.

In 1866, she slipped on ice and was severely injured. The attending doctor gave her little chance for recovery as her condition worsened. Eddy took solace in the Bible, where she read of the healing powers of Jesus Christ, while disdaining the medicine she was given. In an epiphany she felt herself having a spiritual breakthrough that led to her recovery. Later on she wrote, "I can look back and see that at the time of the accident although I had no faith in medicine and did not take it. I had faith that God could raise me up. Hence the effect of the Scripture that I read which strengthened my faith and its results in my recovery."

Subsequently she renewed her research to gain a greater insight into her healing. The concept of spiritual healing and the relationship between mind and body soon emerged. By the close of 1866 she decided that "all causation was Mind, and every effect a mental phenomenon." In effect, she concluded that a patient's beliefs can play a significant part in the healing process.

The following year she began spreading the word about her beliefs in the science of Christian healing that she termed "Christian Science." She also tested her theory by "healing" other people, including some considered incurable. Adherents to the new faith accepted the premise of relying on spiritual rather than medical or material means to bring about cures.

In 1875 she published the first edition of *Science & Health with Key to the Scriptures.* In later years she continued to rework this manuscript in various editions. The book, translated into many languages, has been a best seller for over a century. Disappointed that the Christian church at the time didn't accept her beliefs, she secured a charter and began her church in Boston in 1879. She served as the church's pastor for nearly a decade and as pastor emeritus after her retirement. Other women were allowed to serve as pastors at a time when women still couldn't vote and were generally not found either in pulpits or the medical profession. Pastors tended to utilize passages from the Bible and her works in their sermons.

To further the spread of Christian Science, in 1881 she established the Massachusetts Metaphysical College, the first college of its type in the U.S. She taught there herself for over seven years while also serving as president. The college was closed in 1889. In 1883, Eddy started a monthly magazine, *The Christian Science Journal,* and served as its editor. The *Journal* is still in publication today.

Her ideas throughout her life, and afterward, were and are considered radical by many in social as well as medical and theological circles. She was forced to move many times, and once found all of her belongings tossed on the street. But she kept working to promulgate Christian Science as a method of practical spirituality and prayer-based healing that can be applied to everyday lives and crises. Even in her retirement she continued to exercise a strong influence on the church.

Her writings include *Retrospective & Introspection,* which came out in 1891, when she was 70, *Miscellaneous Writings* in 1896 and *Messages to the Church,* a series in 1900, 1901, and 1902.

Among her many honors was induction into the National Women's Hall of Fame in 1995 and being named in 1998 as one of the 25 "most significant religious figures for Americans in the 20th century" by *Religion & Ethics Weekly*. In 2002 the Mary Baker Library for the Betterment of Humanity opened, with the institution recognized by Congress. Her basic book was chosen by the National Women's Book Association as one of "75 books by women whose words have changed the world." Today, in an even greater tribute, there are local branch churches in over 70 countries around the world.

Eddy died in December 1910 at the age of 89 at Chestnut Hill outside of Boston.

Her many quotes include:

> *"Spirit is the real and eternal,*
> *matter is the unreal and temporal."*

> *"True prayer is not asking God for love; it is learning to love,*
> *and to include all mankind in one affection."*

> *"Sin makes its own hell, and goodness its own heaven."*

> *"I would no more quarrel with a man because of his religion*
> *than I would because of his art."*

> *"Truth is immortal; error is mortal."*

> *"Give up the belief that mind is,*
> *even temporarily, compressed within the skull,*
> *and you will quickly become more manly or womanly.*
> *You will understand yourself and your Maker better than before."*

John Muir
1838–1914

"The power of imagination makes us infinite."

One of the great champions of protecting our natural habitat—forests, mountains, and waterways—John Muir helped create the conservation movement and America's national parks. Protection of the Yosemite area in California and establishment of the Sierra Club, an environmental organization that led to the modern ecology cause, were among his many notable accomplishments. His long career saw him continuing his efforts well past his 65th birthday.

Muir, whose career encompassed being an environmentalist, naturalist, scientist and writer, consistently put forward the principle of how each component of nature was connected to other elements, and that wilderness areas had to be preserved as a unit and not in a fragmentary way. One of his notable quotes was, "When we try to pick out anything by itself, we find it hitched to everything else in the universe."

Born in Dunbar, Scotland in 1838, Muir and his family emigrated to Wisconsin when he was quite young. After some studies at the University of Wisconsin he took to the road or the so-called "university of the wilderness." He walked to Florida and would have continued by sea, as planned, to South America if it weren't for a touch of malaria. Instead he boarded a ship to California and arrived in San Francisco in March 1868 at the age of 30.

Learning of a beautiful range called Yosemite, he decided to see it for himself. He was immediately captivated, and later wrote, "Yosemite is the grandest of all special temples of Nature."

Muir stayed in the area working as a ferry operator, sheepherder, and saw mill operator. He also began developing his theories about nature and its preservation.

In opposition to the belief at the time that Yosemite was created by an earthquake, Muir argued that glaciers had sculpted the distinctive features of the area. In 1871 he found proof of an active glacier, which helped his theory gain acceptance.

Muir roamed around the area, making field studies. He also began his writing in the 1870s, with his work becoming widely published, especially in *The Century Magazine* in New York. This led in turn to his meeting various luminaries who came to Yosemite, including the famed writer and philosopher Ralph Waldo Emerson.

The discovery of a sign illegally claiming private ownership and of loggers cutting down giant sequoia trees triggered his fervent resolve to find ways to protect the area. Danger, he felt, also came from grazing livestock. He termed domestic sheep "hooved locusts." Muir also, to some extent, was ahead of his time in appreciation of wildlife. In advance of the animal rights movement, he challenged hunting as sport, calling it the "murder business."

Eventually he found sufficient support in Congress in 1890 for a bill creating a national park in part of the Yosemite area, but the park was to be under state management, which Muir lamented. In 1892 he helped start the Sierra Club, stating, "Let us do something to make the mountains glad." He became its first president, a position he held for 22 years until his death. The more famous he became as a proponent of conservation, the more articles he had published—and, ironically, the more time he spent away from Yosemite dealing with editors, giving talks, etc.

In 1903, the year Muir turned 65, President Teddy Roosevelt visited the park. The two spent a substantial amount of time touring the valley. Muir managed to convince Roosevelt that the valley's resources were being exploited and that federal management was warranted. In 1905 Muir's objective was reached, with Congress transferring Yosemite into the park.

His next struggle came with the plan to dam part of the Hetch Hetchy Valley/Tuolumne River as a water reservoir for San Francisco. Muir called the valley a "second Yosemite." But after a national debate on the issue, President Woodrow Wilson signed the dam bill into law in 1913.

In his 70s and still very energetic, Muir captured his life well when a question arose about his occupation during an interview while on a trip in South America. "Tramp. I'm 74, and still good at it."

His books included *Picturesque California & the Region West of the Rocky Mountains from Alaska to Mexico*, *The Mountains of California* and *Our National Parks*. Other post-65 books were *Stickeen*, *The Yosemite* and *The Story of Boyhood and Youth*. His book *Travels in Alaska* appeared posthumously in 1915.

Among many tributes are areas named after him including the John Muir Trail and John Muir Wilderness in California and the Muir Glacier at Sitadaka, Alaska. Muir College is part of the University of California at San Diego. Perhaps his greatest tribute comes in the more than 100 million visitors who have come to view Yosemite National Park, a giant 189-mile area of enormous beauty that straddles the western slopes of the Sierra Nevada mountains in California.

Still writing to further his goals, Muir passed away on Dec. 14, 1914.

A tablet set into a rock at Mt. Rubidoux, California reads:

Climb the mountains and get their good tidings. Nature's peace will flow into you as sunshine flows into the trees. The winds will blow their own freshness into you and the storms their energy; while cares will drop off you like autumn leaves.

Among his other memorable quotes were:

"Until he extends the circle of his compassion to all living things, man will not himself find peace."

"Everybody needs beauty as well as bread, places to play in and pray in, where nature may heal and give strength to body and soul alike."

"Any fool can destroy trees. They can't run away, and if they could, they would still be destroyed, chased and hunted down as long as fun or a dollar could be got out of their bark hides."

"The clearest way into the Universe is through a forest wilderness."

"No synonym for God is so perfect as beauty."

"In God's wildness lies the hope of the world."

Andrew Carnegie
1835–1919

"The man who dies rich dies disgraced."

Andrew Carnegie, an industrialist and philanthropist, lived up to his own statement in a sense, having divested himself of a considerable amount of his riches by the time of his death. With the sale of his steel company in 1900 for $480 million, when he was 65, he became the richest man in the world. Before he passed away in 1919 he had given about $350 million to various causes. But Carnegie wasn't fond of charities and believed in institutions that helped people to help themselves. He was also unusual among persons of great wealth by believing that in "taxing estates heavily at death, the state marks the condemnation of the selfish millionaire's unworthy life."

Overall, Carnegie donated around 90 percent of his fortune to cultural, scientific and educational institutions for the "improvement of mankind." He tried to make his efforts in philanthropy as efficient as his methods of conducting business.

Among the institutions indebted to Carnegie's philanthropy, all created after he was 65, are the Carnegie Institute of Washington in 1902, the Carnegie Hero Fund Commission in 1904, the Carnegie Foundation for the Advancement of Teaching in 1905, and the Carnegie Endowment for International Peace in 1910. He also set up the lesser known Church Peace Union, with members from various religions. One of his last philanthropic trusts was to the Carnegie Corporation in 1911.

He funded the Palace of Peace in The Hague, the Netherlands, which had its grand opening in 1913 and evolved into the World Court. His financial awards gave birth to over 2,800 libraries throughout the English-speaking world. The sign above the Carnegie Library in Pittsburgh reads: "Free to the Public." When he learned that blacks were unable to use libraries in the South, he financed special libraries for African Americans.

Before he turned 65 he helped in the creation of Carnegie Hall in New York in 1892. He also assisted in formation of the Carnegie Institute of Technology in Pittsburgh in 1900.

Carnegie, who rose from rags to riches, saw value in being born poor, saying, "The richest heritage a young man can have is to be born into poverty."

While evolving into a great philanthropist, Carnegie was also considered by many to be one of the robber barons who emerged in the rapid industrialization of the U.S. during the latter part of the 19th century. Moreover, his beneficence in his latter years had to be reconciled with dubious business practices and harsh labor conditions for workers in the factories that led to his wealth. His strike-breaking policy led to one of the most vicious battles in the history of the labor movement in the U.S. at the Homestead Steel Mill in Pennsylvania in 1892. Carnegie, who often seemed conflicted about his wealth and the issue of labor versus management, was accused of hypocrisy by many observers.

Carnegie was born in 1835 in Dunfermline, Scotland. His father was a weaver; industrialization sealed the fate of his trade. The family emigrated to Allegheny (now Pittsburgh) in Pennsylvania in 1848. The 13-year-old youth worked in a cotton mill for as much as 12 hours a day for $1.20 a week, while also going to night school. Subsequently, he worked as a messenger in a telegraph office. He caught the attention of an executive at the Pennsylvania Railroad, where he went to work, and his rise was rapid. By 1859, at 24, he had become superintendent of the Pittsburgh division of the railroad.

Carnegie made excellent investments in sleeping cars and oil interests, accumulating some capital. He foresaw that the onslaught of industrialization would mean greater use of steel. He began buying firms involved in steel production and consolidated them into the Carnegie Steel Company. He was a millionaire at an early age, operating with the motto "watch costs and the profits take care of themselves." He also made shrewd use of an improved accounting system, and sped up traffic through his vertically integrated system to maximize production. By

1900 the company produced about one quarter of all the steel made in the U.S.

Carnegie was adroit in venture capitalism and an excellent salesman. The latter was aided by skillful use of his Scottish accent and storytelling ability.

Carnegie reflected a dichotomy of sorts when it came to labor. On paper, he favored the right of laborers to create unions, which was unusual among his fellow "Captains of Industry." However, when push came to shove in the bloody Homestead Strike of 1892, his support did go to management.

Finally succumbing to his desire for retirement, Carnegie sold his company to financier J.P. Morgan for $480 million (over $12 billion today) in 1900, when he was 65. The sale made him the world's richest man.

Carnegie married his wife, Louise, in 1886. They bought an estate in Scotland, where they lived for part of the year. An anti-imperialist and a member of the Anti-Imperialist League, which developed after the Spanish-American War of 1898, Carnegie went as far as offering the Philippines $20 million to buy their independence—$20 million being the amount the U.S. was going to pay Spain to purchase the islands.

Even before World War I Carnegie advocated the establishment of a world organization like the League of Nations. While a pacifist to some extent, profits being profits, his company still made armor plate for the U.S. Navy, as well as other navies. The advent of the first world war was said to have greatly depressed him in light of his efforts—even meetings with Kaiser Wilhelm of Germany in 1907 and 1912—to prevent the conflict. Despite his prior pacifism, he finally decided that the U.S. was right to enter the war as a means to construct a peace between nations.

He died in 1919 at his Massachusetts estate. When he was nearly 80 Carnegie commented on his life, "...when I go for a trial for the things done on Earth, I think I'll get a 'Not Guilty' verdict through my efforts to make the Earth a little better than I found it."

Carnegie explained his philosophy in his *Autobiography, Triumphant Democracy,* and *Gospels of Wealth.* In the latter he wrote: "This, then, is held to be the duty of the man of wealth: first, to set an example of unostentatious living, shunning display; to provide moderately for the legitimate wants of those dependent upon him; and, after doing so, to consider all surplus revenues which come to him simply as trust funds which he is strictly bound as a matter of duty to administer in the manner which, in his judgment, is best calculated to produce the most beneficial results for the community."

Overall, Carnegie wrote eight books and many articles. He had a number of his speeches—he was said to have not used ghostwriters—published as pamphlets.

Among his more memorable quotes:

"It is more difficult to give money away intelligently than it is to earn it in the first place."

"It is the mind that makes the body rich."

"Take care of your pennies and the pounds will take care of themselves."

"Anything in life worth having is worth working for."

"You can't push anyone up a ladder unless he is willing to climb a little."

"The first man gets the oyster, the second man gets the shell."

"No amount of ability is of the slightest avail without honor."

Alexander Graham Bell

1847–1922

"Concentrate all your thoughts on the task at hand. The sun's rays do not burn until brought to a focus."

Shortly before he died, Alexander Graham Bell said, "There cannot be mental atrophy in any person who continues to observe, to remember what he observes, and to seek answers for his unceasing hows and whys about things."

A visionary to the end, Bell's life was the embodiment of this belief. Best known for his invention of the telephone, he was busy working on other inventions well past his 65th birthday. At the age of 75, a year before his death, he received a patent on a watercraft, a hydrofoil, considered to be the fastest in the world. He also designed, on a theoretical basis, a machine for sorting punch-coded cards in a project for the U.S. Census Bureau. The projected use of binary systems of computation come close to the principles of modern day computers.

In his home he came up with an early kind of air conditioning by having fans blow current of air over large blocks of ice. He was also interested in the process of desalinization and water distillation, even converting human breath into water. Conversion of garbage and alcohol into fuel were other projects. The notion of utilizing solar panels to warm houses was another idea he conceived. Flying machines with telephones was still another dream, and in 1893 he came up with a diagram for a jet engine.

Bell was also a pioneer of aviation through his experiments with kites, rockets, and jet power. "The more I experiment, the more convinced I become that flying machines are practical."

Well ahead of his time, Bell warned of non-renewable energy sources, with his words sounding prophetic today. "We can take coal out of a mine, but we can never put it back. We can draw oil from subterranean reservoirs, but we can never fill them again."

Sheep-breeding experiments that Bell began continued after his death. He crossbred sheep with an extra set of nipples in expectation of generating more births of twins and thus increasing the available amount of meat and wool. Had he more time, there is no telling what other inventions Bell might have contributed.

Despite increasingly poor health—pre-insulin diabetes and an ironic partial loss of hearing—he continued experimenting, lecturing, and traveling.

Bell was born in Edinburgh, Scotland, to a family heavily involved in communication, especially for the deaf. His father had devised a system of "visible speech" to teach the deaf to talk through the symbolic representation of the use of currents of air over lips, tongue and throat in articulating sounds. In 1870 Bell migrated to Branford in the province of Ontario in Canada. Later he moved on to Boston, where he lectured to teachers of the deaf and ran his own school of vocal physiology. In 1872 he established a school for the deaf in Boston that eventually became part of Boston University, where he was appointed a professor of vocal physiology.

The invention of the telephone in 1876, when he was only 29, stemmed from Bell's research into ways to improve the telegraph. Others were working on the same invention, but Bell was the first to receive a patent (by a scant two hours). The patent, which cost $15, is considered one of the most valuable patents ever issued in the U.S. or elsewhere. The first patent was for an improvement in telegraphy, with a second patent in 1877 actually calling the invention a "telephone." The device, based on transmitting sound by electricity, was initially termed an "electrical speech machine." He worked with a young mechanic, Thomas Watson, and the first telephone message was to his associate in a nearby room: "Mr. Watson...come here...I need you."

News of his invention spread quickly. The first demonstrations came at the 1876 Centennial Exposition in Philadelphia, and before the American Academy of Arts & Sciences in Boston in 1877. By 1878 the first telephone exchange was set up in New Haven, Connecticut, and by 1884 long distance connections were established between Boston and New York. New York had the honor of the first pay phone, in 1889. A trans-Atlantic phone line came in 1915.

In 1877 Bell married his wife, Mabel, and in 1882 became an American citizen. Not long after his great invention Bell wrote to his father: "The day is coming when telegraph wires will be laid on houses just like water or gas…and friends will converse with each other without leaving home."

In 1878 President Rutherford Hayes was the first U.S. president to talk on the telephone at the White House. His first call was to Bell, who was only a few miles away.

Bell won France's Volta Prize and some 50,000 francs (about $10,000) in 1880 for his invention of the telephone. He used the money to establish a laboratory in Boston, where he and his associates proceeded to work on new inventions. Among these were:

- An audiometer used to measure sound levels in hearing.

- A photophone that transmits speech on beams of light rays (Bell considered the photophone, which paved the way for future work on laser and fiber optic communications, to be "the greatest invention I have ever made, greater than the telephone.")

- An induction balance used to find metallic objects in the human body. (This device, however, failed to locate a bullet in President Garfield's body after he was shot by an assassin on July 2, 1881. Later, it was discovered the reason for the failure was that Garfield was lying on a bed with metal springs that deflected the machine.) Bell developed this concept further with a device called a "telephone probe," which was capable of making a telephone receiver click when it touched metal.

- The first wax recording cylinder or stylus, which helped create the underlying basis for the phonograph.

- The graphophone, the first successful sound recorder.

The invention of the telephone led to organization of the Bell Telephone Company, which eventually became AT&T, in 1877. At one early point he was faced with litigation by a rival company over the rights to the telephone, but the Supreme Court upheld Bell's claim.

Overall, Bell faced over 500 patent lawsuits.

In 1881, due to the tragedy of a newborn son who died from respiratory problems, Bell designed a metal vacuum jacket to facilitate breathing. This device was the forerunner of the iron lung used to help polio victims in the 1950s.

Bell was influential in the creation of the magazine *Science* in 1880. The publication later became the official organ of the American Association for the Advancement of Science. He became president of the National Geographic Society 1898–1903, and a regent of the Smithsonian Institution in 1898.

After the turn of the century Bell became increasingly interested in aviation. His study of flight began with creating a tetrahedron (a solid figure with four triangular faces) kite. He and associates developed the aileron, a moveable section of a plane's wing that can control roll. In 1907, four years after the Wright Brothers flew their plane at Kitty Hawk, N.C., Bell and his associates produced an aircraft. In 1909 their "Silver Dart" flew for half a mile and became the first successful powered flight in Canada. (Bell had established a summer home he called Beinn Bhreagh—"beautiful mountain" in Gaelic—at Baddeck on Cape Breton Island in Nova Scotia.)

Bell and his group also started work on hydrofoil boats, which travel above water level at high speeds. In 1917, during World War I, the U.S. War Department was looking for designs for motorboats to help protect submarines. Bell argued that a hydrofoil could successfully skim over a mine-laden body of water. In 1919, when he was 67, his group developed a hydrofoil that held the world speed record until 1963.

Eugenics, the field of "improving" the human race by controlling the mating of people and thus weeding out perceived defective characteristics, also drew Bell's interest. He was said to have calculated that a eugenically sound mother should or could bear ten children.

Bell died on Aug. 2, 1922 at Baddeck, where a museum displaying many of his original inventions is run by the Canadian government. A plaque at the museum states, "The inventor is a man who looks upon the world and is not contented with things as they are. He wants to improve whatever he sees, he wants to benefit the world."

Bell's funeral on Aug. 4, 1922 was said to be marked by having every phone in North America (more than 10 million by this time) become silent for a minute's tribute.

His advice to other inventors was summed up with these quotes:

*"Leave the beaten path occasionally
and dive into the woods.
Every time you do so
you will be certain to find something
that you have never seen before.
Follow it up, explore all around it,
and before you know it,
you will have something worth thinking about
to occupy your mind.
All really big discoveries
are the results of thought."*

*"Man is an animal which, alone among the animals,
refuses to be satisfied by the fulfillment of animal desires."*

"The achievement of one goal should be the starting point of another."

*"When one door closes, another opens;
but we often look so long and regretfully upon the closed door
that we do not see the one which has opened for us."*

*"What the power is I cannot say; all I know is that it exists
and it becomes available only when a man is in that state of mind
in which he knows exactly what he wants
and is fully determined not to quit until he finds it."*

Sarah Bernhardt
1844–1923

"Life begets life. Energy creates energy. It is by spending oneself that one becomes rich."

Despite the amputation of a leg in 1914 when she was 70, Sarah Bernhardt—acclaimed by many as the greatest actress of her era, and known to adoring fans as "the divine Sarah"—continued to act, demonstrating her emotional range with a voice described as "silvery." She even entertained troops at the front during World War I. For a while she acted from a specially designed sedan chair, and then she was equipped with an artificial leg. Meanwhile, she kept acting around the world while also managing her own theater in Paris until her death in 1923. Her last stage performance, when she was already 78, was in *La Gloire* by Maurice Rostand in 1922.

Throughout her lengthy career, and particularly to offset the ravages of age and accidents, she lived up to her motto of *"quand meme,"* which means, more or less, "in spite of it all."

Bernhardt became the first great actress to appear in the new medium of film, starring in 1911 (at a mere 67) in *La Reine Elizabeth* and *La Dame aux Camellias (The Lady of the Camellias)*. The latter play was most associated with her, and she continued performing it until 1914, when she was 70. Thereafter she kept playing the letter and death scene of the main character, Marguerite Gautier, the redeemed courtesan. In the U.S., the play was often shortened to *Camille,* though there is no such character in the work.

She conducted her last tour of the U.S. in 1916, traveling in a private railway termed the "Sarah Bernhardt Special." In 1918, already 74, she started a European tour, playing parts she could act while seated.

Bernhardt was born in Paris on Oct. 23, 1844 as the illegitimate child of French-Dutch parents. As she was partly of Jewish descent on her mother's side (her mother was said to be a courtesan), she suffered anti-Semitic slurs throughout her career. Despite her Jewish background, she was put in a convent and raised as a Catholic. At one point she wanted to be a nun, though she was said to have shocked some nuns with her less than church-like language. With the help of one of her mother's lovers, a nobleman, she entered the Paris Conservatory to study acting at 13. While not accounted a brilliant or promising student, she made her stage debut at the Theatre Francais (later known as the Comedie Francaise) on Sept. 1, 1862 in Racine's *Imphigenie en Aulide.*

She attained a measure of stardom in the 1870s, with her most popular role *The Lady of the Camellias.* Her reputation was firmly established by her role as Zanetto, the wandering minstrel in Francois Coppee's *Le Passant.* She later scored a great success as the queen in Victor Hugo's *Ruy Blas.*

She left the Theatre Francais after an argument (she slapped the face of a senior actress) and tried the world of burlesque, which turned out not to be her métier. She also had an illegitimate son, Maurice—her only child—when she was 20, the result of an affair with a Belgian nobleman, Henri, Prince of Ligne. Returning to the theater, she continued acting and was acclaimed as France's most notable actress. Eleanor Duse was her major competition as far as world-wide honors. In 1880, after a successful acting season in London, she ended her relationship with what was then called the Comedie Francaise and started an independent career with the first of a sextet of acting tours throughout the U.S. Marriage to a Greek actor in 1882 ended after a year with his death from drugs. In 1898 she bought the Theatre des Nations in Paris and renamed it the Theatre Sarah Bernhardt.

Sought after by many men, she had several love affairs. Her lovers may have included Victor Hugo and even the Prince of Wales, the future Edward VII, King of England. Marcel Proust used her character as the actress Berma in his great work *Remembrance of Things Past.*

Despite less than accolades from some critics for her curious roles—such as playing a boy when she was already middle-aged in Edmond Rostand's *L'Aiglon*—her plays and performances were generally successful, commercially and otherwise. She also played Joan of Arc, a

19 year old, when she was 65. In one of her more unusual tributes, she was known as the only actress to successfully portray both Ophelia and Hamlet in Shakespeare's *Hamlet.*

In discussing male parts, she said in her posthumous 1924 treatise, *The Art of the Theatre:* "I have often been asked why I am so fond of playing male parts. As a matter of fact, it is not male parts, but male brains that I prefer."

In 1905, while performing in Rio de Janeiro, she suffered an injury to her right knee while jumping from a parapet during a performance of *Tosca.* By 1911 she was unable to walk without support, and she was carried about in a litter chair. A few years later the leg was amputated due to gangrene. But she kept acting and managing her theatre, and found time to show that her artistic gifts included writing and sculpture. Some of her plays were published, as well as her memoirs, *Ma Double Vie* in 1907. An autobiographical novel, *The Idol of Paris,* came out in 1920, when she was 76. She also provided "guidance"—though others felt her comments suggested revisions—to playwrights trying to write plays for her.

As a retreat, she spent many of her latter years at a complex she bought and developed at Belle Ile en Mer ("Beautiful Island in the Sea"), a small island off the coast of Brittany in France.

She was faithful, if not to lovers, then to her belief that continuing to work was healthy, though she suffered from a kidney disease. She kept at her tasks until her last days, when she was even involved in her eighth film, *La Voyante (The Eaglet).* She was a world-wide celebrity, enjoying attention and accolades during her 60 years on stage and screen. She even had herself photographed, quite prematurely, in a coffin when she was only 35. Her popularity led to many product endorsements ranging from face creams to real estate.

To the doctors attending her on her death bed, she said, "Even if I leave, I have done my duty, and the world will not forget." Her funeral in Paris was a major event, attended by many luminaries. One estimate was that as many as one million people lined the streets for her funeral cortege, which went past her theater.

In one of many tributes, Mark Twain commented, "There are five kinds of actresses, bad actresses, fair actresses, good actresses, great actresses—and then there is Sarah Bernhardt."

In summing up, Bernhardt wrote:

> *"A fond farewell to this theatrical world I've known.*
> *It's filled with thespian tragedies which I shall no longer strut so proudly*
> *upon this stage as I portray all women's loneliness*
> *within this world of angry men..."*

> *"Legend remains victorious in spite of history."*

> *"One should hate very little, because it's extremely fatiguing."*

Thomas Alva Edison
1847–1931

"Genius is one percent inspiration,
ninety nine percent perspiration."

Thomas Edison is credited with being one of the greatest inventors in the history of mankind. He patented more than one thousand separate inventions in over eight decades, the most patents ever given to anyone.

His inventions led to the formation of major industries and major lifestyle changes in the U.S. and around the world. Yet for most of his life he suffered from seriously impaired hearing, noting many years later that he "hadn't heard a bird sing" since he was 12. He compensated for his handicap with his creativity and hard work, continuing well past his 65th birthday and into his early 80s. He set up a laboratory at Menlo Park, N.J. (he was dubbed the "Wizard of Menlo Park") where he and his assistants labored on projects. The Menlo Park laboratory, tailored for research and development, was the prototype of the modern research facility.

One of Edison's credos was, "Many of life's failures are people who did not realize how close they were to success when they gave up." His life was an example, as he had explored many theories about electric light before his experiments worked. Patents were one thing, but the real effort came in "the long, laborious trouble of working them out and producing apparatus which is commercial."

One of his major projects after 65—though troubled by diabetes, stomach disorders, an ear abscess and resultant operations—was a search for an alternative source of natural rubber. In 1917 he began conducting experiments for the U.S. Navy, with over 40 ideas in various stages of planning, none of which were ever adopted. Among his innovations were a submarine detection device and new sea anchors for quick turnarounds to avoid torpedoes. In attempting to handle his own health to some extent he dabbled in dietary matters, possibly damaging himself with an insufficient intake of fluids. In the 1920s he suggested a method of changing standard banking/finance methods which involved, among other factors, using commodities as reserve instead of gold.

World-famous for inventions that changed lifestyles dramatically, Edison was sought for his opinions on many subjects beyond inventions and science, though some quibbled that he took full credit for some inventions that others had worked on. As another token of respect, his work also inspired some science fiction writers.

In discussing the city of the future, he predicted that the saving of time will be of primary importance, with congestion solved by mathematicians. Furthermore, "...crime will decrease before the advent of the scientific policeman, and taxes will become astonishingly low with government of the cities by experts." He also opined that "Scientific men as a rule do not believe in the immortality of the soul because the more they investigate the works of nature the more firmly they reach that conclusion." One prediction—that radios would fail to make a major mark—obviously turned out differently.

Edison was born in Milan, Ohio in 1847. He had little formal education. One reason: In what can be considered one of the most faulty academic assessments ever made, a schoolmaster thought he was "retarded," or at least slow.

Edison's first invention, an electric vote recorder, came when he was only 21. This invention didn't enhance his financial situation. But another invention, a stock ticker system, was sold for $40,000, quite a fortune in those days. In coming years he became both wealthy and famous.

He patented the phonograph in 1877, and developed the incandescent light bulb in 1879. Moreover, he set up the initial distribution company that transported electrical energy into private homes, preparing the groundwork for a huge industry.

Edison was a brilliant inventor, but he also possessed strong marketing and entrepreneurial skills. It was not sufficient, he thought, to just invent something; it had to have a commercial use. "There is a wide difference between completing an invention and putting the manufactured article on the market," he said. Accordingly, Edison became involved in manufacturing himself, and participated in the creation of several companies. The most important one eventually became General Electric.

Other key inventions were a motion picture camera known as the kinetograph (the first rudimentary machine to effectively capture objects in motion) and projector, a dictating machine, mimeograph machine, and a storage battery. He also worked on the development of silent movies in the 1890s, synthetic chemicals, mining machinery, waxed paper, a mimeograph, and a long playing record. To secure an independent source of rubber for the U.S. he conducted a search in 1928 for a new sort of supply.

Edison also overcame the ravages of a major 1914 fire that destroyed much of his West Orange, NJ research complex and his work. Undaunted, Edison said, "I am 67, but I'm not too old to make a fresh start."

His fame made him a spokesman on many subjects, including foreign alliances and prohibition. He was not loath to give his opinion, some of which elicited considerable criticism. On the subject of religion he said, "I have never seen the slightest scientific proof of the religious theories of heaven and hell, of future life for individuals, or of a personal God. I do not know the soul, I know the mind. If there is really any soul I have found no evidence of it in my investigations…but I have found repeatedly evidence of mind…I do not believe in the God of the theologians; but that there is a Supreme Intelligence, I do not doubt."

In 1921 Edison devised what was dubbed the "Edison Questionnaire," a factual quiz for applicants who wanted to work in his laboratories. Few passed the quiz, also termed the "Ignoramometer," and the exam was widely ridiculed. Undaunted, Edison came up with a new test the next year which, to some extent, was the prototype of the more modern personality tests some corporations use with jobseekers.

Painstaking, Edison accumulated over 2,000 notebooks on his ideas and how to bring these concepts to practical fruition. The Congressional Medal of Honor was awarded to him in 1928.

Very much in favor of out-of-the-box methods, Edison focused on practical results. When a technician in his lab was stymied using eminently reasonable methods to solve a problem, Edison exclaimed, "Thank God you can't think up any more reasonable things, so you'll have to begin thinking up unreasonable things to try and now you'll hit the solution in no time."

Edison was married twice, and had three children with each wife. He died in West Orange, N.J. in 1931 and received many public and governmental tributes. Under the impetus of President Herbert Hoover, electric lights were shut off for one minute (mostly in private residences) on the day of his funeral as a special honor commemorating his life's work.

Among his sayings:

"Everything comes to him who hustles while he waits."

"Hell, there are no rules here—we're trying to accomplish something."

"Opportunity is missed by most people because it is dressed in overalls and looks like work."

"Results! Why, man, I have gotten lots of results. I know several thousand things that won't work."

"There is no expedient to which a man will not go to avoid the labor of thinking."

"We don't know a millionth of one percent about anything."

Oliver Wendell Holmes, Jr.
1841–1935

"A moment's insight
is sometimes worth a lifetime's experience."

In 1933, when Oliver Wendell Holmes, Jr. was 92 and had only retired two years before as Chief Justice of the U.S. Supreme Court, he was paid a courtesy visit by president-elect Franklin D. Roosevelt. Found reading Plato in Greek, Holmes was asked why by a somewhat surprised Roosevelt. Holmes replied, "Why, to improve my mind."

This anecdote captures the spirit and intellectual acuity of Holmes, a soldier, jurist and philosopher who was considered by many to have been the most influential judge in the English-speaking world. In his many decisions Holmes interpreted the Constitution in the light of specific social events, experiences and needs rather than as inviolable abstract principles. "Law," he wrote, "should develop along with the society it serves."

Facts in a changing world, he insisted, should be examined by the Supreme Court instead of arbitrarily relying on static concepts. He also explained his position by stating "that the best test of truth is the power of the thought to get itself accepted in the competition of the market, and that truth is the only ground upon which their wishes can be carried out. That, at any rate, is the theory of our Constitution. It is an experiment, as all life is an experiment."

In the same vein, he wrote in *The Path of the Law* that "It is revolting to have no better reason for a rule of law than that it was laid down in the time of Henry IV. It is still more revolting if the grounds upon which it was laid down have vanished long since, and the rule simply persists from blind imitation of the past."

His opinions, often at odds with his fellow justices, led to him being dubbed "The Great Dissenter." Actually, in around a thousand decisions, only 72 involved a dissent, less than some other justices in the history of the Supreme Court.

Holmes was responsible for clarifications for limiting free speech, guaranteed under the First Amendment. This came about in the *Schench v. U.S.* case. Congress had passed the Espionage Act and Sedition Act in 1917–18 during World War I, and a number of cases soon surfaced involving free speech and the First Amendment. Holmes supported the new laws, but finally came out with his famed test of whether any act by a person reached the level of creating "a clear and present danger" and thus violation of the laws. In a much-quoted and common sense application, he said no one had a right to falsely cry "Fire!" in a crowded theater.

A decision that would be far more controversial today came over the issue of eugenics, the field of "improving" humanity by controlling mating of people. In *Buck v. Bell* in 1927 he upheld the constitutionality of a Virginia law that allowed sterilization of patients/residents of state mental facilities if they were classified as "mental defectives," arguing "three generations of imbeciles are enough."

In the *Lochner* case in 1905, the Court held by a vote of 5–4 that a New York State law limiting the hours of work in bakeries to no more than 10 hours a day was unconstitutional. Holmes dissented, and his position has since been validated

In his 1881 book *The Common Law*, comprising a series of lectures delivered at Harvard, he questioned many of the fundamental theories of Anglo-American law. His *Collected Legal Papers* were published in 1920. In his will, Holmes donated over $250,000 to the U.S., with this sum eventually utilized to commission a series of books on the Supreme Court's history duly titled the *Oliver Wendell Holmes Devise History.*

Holmes was appointed to the Supreme Court by President Teddy Roosevelt in 1901 when he was 61. When he retired in 1932 after 30 years on the bench—most of it when he was past 65—he became the oldest man to have ever served on the Court. Until he was over 85, Holmes would walk to and from the Court when it was in session, a distance of about two miles each way.

In addition to his respect and reverence for the law, Holmes greatly admired the service given by soldiers. His position stemmed from his experiences in the Civil War, in which he was severely wounded three times at such bloody battles as Antietam and Chancellorsville. His famed 1895 Memorial Day speech, "The Soldier's Faith," contained lines from a favorite poem, "Soldier Buried on the Battlefield." In an earlier Memorial Day speech he spoke of how "in our youth, our hearts were touched with fire."

After the Civil War, where his rank had risen from lieutenant to a brevet colonel, Holmes—who was born in Boston—decided to devote his career to the law. He quickly rose to become a member of the Massachusetts Supreme Court, where he served 20 years.

Many students of the law made special visits to Washington, D.C. and the Supreme Court to see Holmes on the bench. To one young student he was reputed to have said, "Young man, the secret of my success is that at an early age I discovered that I was not God." In a similar vein, he opined, "As long as one writes decisions he is concerned with the future and never can be sure that he won't find out that he really is a damn fool after all."

To another young man, he said, "You make me chuckle when you say that you are no longer young, that you have turned 24. A man is or may be young after 60, and not old before 80."

And when catching a glimpse of an attractive girl's legs when ninety, he quipped, "Oh, to be 70 again!"

Far from being sentimental, Holmes once wrote a friend, "I have had thoughts on the need of a society for the promotion of hard-heartedness." He added at another time, "To know is not less than to feel."

The Internal Revenue Service building in the nation's capital bears another of his quotes: "Taxes are the price we pay for a civilized society."

On his 90th birthday Holmes gave a radio talk in response to tributes from members and leaders of the American bar. The essence of his philosophy might be summed up in these lines: "The race is over, but the work never is done while the power to work remains. To live is to function; that is all there is to living."

After retiring from the Supreme Court at 90, he lived until two days before his 94th birthday, passing away on March 6, 1935. He was buried in Arlington National Cemetery. A 1935 movie entitled *The Magnificent Yankee* was made about his life and his work.

Among many other memorable quotes:

"Lawyers spend a great deal of time shoveling smoke."

"A man is usually more careful of his money than his principles."

*"To have doubted one's own first principles
is the mark of a civilized man."*

*"We should be eternally vigilant against attempts
to check the expression of opinions that we loathe."*

*"…a man is pretty sure to get his due share of appreciation,
for whether he speaks or is silent, the world generally finds him out."*

*"The main part of intellectual education is not the acquisition of facts
but learning how to make facts live."*

Sigmund Freud
1856–1939

"In small matters trust the mind,
in the large ones the heart."

One of the primary figures of the 20th century, Freud's theories revolutionized the field of psychology and launched psychoanalysis. The word "Freudian" has entered our vocabulary along with such terms as id, ego, superego, unconscious, inferiority complex and libido. If Freud's fate, as he suggested, was "to agitate the sleep of mankind," he was enormously successful.

Freud was born in 1856 in Freiberg, which is about 150 miles north of Vienna and now part of the Czech Republic. Trained as a neurologist, Freud sought to establish a universal theory of behavior and its causes. Sexuality, he deemed, was the root factor in much of human behavior. He stressed the significance of unconscious mental processes, and emphasized repressed sexuality—which began in early childhood—as often being the key motor driving the unconscious mind. He also wrote that " . . . there is an intimate connection between all mental happenings—a fact which guarantees that a psychological discovery even in a remote field will be of unpredictable value in other fields."

Freud posited that the mind had three basic elements: the id, which was the source of instinctive desires/urges; the ego, which provided a link between the private id and the external world/society; and the superego, which processed the learned axioms and practices of society.

In "Some Elementary Lessons In Psychoanalysis," one of his last papers, Freud noted that the existence of the unconscious was far from unknown—writers, for example, had employed the subject—but it had taken his efforts to develop its place in science.

In his early life and studies Freud, who was Jewish, had to contend with anti-Semitism in academic circles and elsewhere. Throughout his life he contended with his identity as a Jew, settling for the most part with being Jewish without any great belief in religion overall.

In 1900 his *Interpretation of Dreams* caused a great stir in the medical field and helped to further the field of psychoanalysis. The use of "psychoanalysis" as a term was first used by him in 1896.

In 1924, when 68, he underwent two operations for cancer of the mouth. The cancer was due to smoking cigars, a habit he still only gave up for brief periods. He had trouble eating. Part of his upper jaw had to be removed and replaced with a metal prosthesis, a procedure that could only be done with a local anesthetic. After the operation he could chew and speak only with difficulty, but he refused to stop smoking, the probable cause of the cancer. He also refused to stop working, both writing and continuing his private practice, which he conducted from 1886 to 1938. Before death in London in 1939 he underwent another two dozen operations, either to remove precancerous tissue or to have his prosthesis cleaned.

Despite these continuing medical problems, he never stopped working. He wrote and treated patients (for $25 an hour). In 1923, the year his cancer appeared, he came out with *The Ego and the Id,* which created great interest. His essays included "The Future of An Illusion" in 1927 and "Female Sexuality" in 1931. Meanwhile, he kept up a voluminous correspondence and continued to see patients. His medical condition, however, preyed on his mind, and he admitted, "I think about the possibility of death every day. It is good practice."

Shortly after his 65th birthday in 1921 he was quoted, "I quite suddenly took a step into real old age. Since then the thought of death has not left me, and sometimes I have the impression that seven of my internal organs are fighting to have the honor of bringing my life to an end."

In London, late in life, he began work on *Moses and Monotheism,* originally conceived as a historical novel in which he claimed Moses was an amalgam of two persons, an Egyptian prince and a Jew, and that the Egyptian had been murdered, a crime that lay at the root of Jewish guilt. Moreover, he wrote that this version of Moses managed to become leader of a Semitic tribe and to convince them to follow a monotheistic religion patterned, to some extent, from the beliefs of the former Pharaoh Akhenaton.

Toward his final days, when he was already 82, he began work on the unfinished *Outline of Psychoanalysis,* which would have presumably rounded out his theories.

Previously, Freud had produced three major "cultural works." The first was *Totem and Taboo,* an exploration of the ancestral past of mankind, which he finished in 1913. He described the book, an attempt to explore the deep ancestral past of mankind, as "the most daring enterprise I have ever ventured."

In 1927 he published *The Future of An Illusion,* a critical study of organized religion. He was skeptical and sometimes hostile to religion. At the end of 1929, as the economic depression deepened, he came out with the third culturally oriented book, *Civilization and Its Discontents.* He developed the idea that society/civilization evolves out of a need to curb the individual's unruly sexual/aggressive appetites. The more suppression of these appetites, the more neuroses. He hoped, in vain, that ethics—the rules of mankind—could benefit from psychoanalytic understanding, especially understanding of the superego or conscience.

While believing that reason can triumph in the world, Freud was far from sanguine about the prospects of civilization in general. "It goes without saying that a civilization which leaves so large a number of its participants unsatisfied and drives them into revolt neither has nor deserves the prospect of a lasting existence."

Many honors came to Freud, but he was disappointed that the Nobel Prize wasn't one of them. One of the problems was difficulty considering his work in mental health under the medical category.

The words "Freudian slip" caught on, though his theories came under greater scrutiny and criticism. In 1924 *The Chicago Tribune* offered him the then-munificent sum of $25,000 to analyze the motivations of Leopold and Loeb, the two university students who murdered a teenager in one of the more famous criminal cases in U.S. history. Freud declined. Later that year Hollywood producer Sam Goldwyn offered even more money, said to be $100,000, for Freud to somehow participate in a film about great love stories of history. Unwilling to have his name used in this commercial fashion, he turned this offer down, too.

Freud was slow to recognize the true horror of the Nazi menace, and initially refused to flee Austria as other Jews did. In 1933 his books, along with those of other Jewish luminaries like Einstein and Kafka, were burned by the Nazis. He was 82 and not well when Austria was swallowed by Germany in 1938. The world worried about his welfare, including President Roosevelt.

Interestingly, the U.S. was hardly one of Freud's favorite countries, probably due to American informality and what he considered to be less than respectful questioning of his theories. In the past, some of his comments had been, "America is gigantic, but a gigantic mistake" and "America is useful for nothing else but to supply money."

Freud wasn't willing to move to London until convinced his children (he had six) would have a better future. Having waited too long to leave, his situation became complicated. Finally, his case went as high as Heinrich Himmler, one of Adolf Hitler's most important officials. At last his emigration papers came, but he had to sign a document affirming that he had been properly treated by the Nazis. He was supposed to have signed and added, "I can most heartily recommend the Gestapo to anyone." A member of the American Legation accompanied him on his trip from Vienna to Paris and then London.

At the age of 82, afflicted with his cancer and a painful prosthesis, he wrote that the quality of being conscious "remains the one light which illuminates our path and leads us through the darkness of mental life."

New lumps appeared in his mouth and throat at the end of 1938 and the start of 1939. He died in September 1939 at the age of 83, three weeks after England declared war on Germany.

Among Freud's comments:

"When inspiration does not come to me, I go halfway to meet it."

"From error to error we discover the entire truth."

*"The great question that has never been answered,
and which I have not yet been able to answer,
despite my thirty years of research into the feminine soul,
is 'What does a woman want?'"*

William Butler Yeats
1865–1939

"Do not wait to strike until the iron is hot,
but make it hot by striking."

William Butler Yeats, a poet and dramatist, was one of the literary stalwarts of the 20th century, and a recipient of the Nobel Prize for Literature in 1923. He was in the forefront of the Irish literary surge, providing substantial impetus for the "Celtic Revival," a movement to confront English/Victorian cultural influences. Promotion of the native heritage of Ireland remained one of his lifelong goals, though he never mastered the Gaelic language himself.

Yeats continued writing well after he was 65, with *The Winding Stair & Other Poems* coming out in 1933 when he was 68, *Wheels and Butterflies* in 1934, *A Full Moon in March* in 1935, and *Last Poems* in 1939, shortly before he was 73. Part of 1938 was spent on working on a play, *The Death of Cuchulain*. In his latter years he also worked on the final version of *A Vision*, a 1925 book written with his wife, Georgie, that combined elements of marriage therapy, the variables of human personality, and occultism.

His poetry turned more serious in his later years, showing considerable pessimism over the foibles of mankind and the deepening political troubles in both Ireland and throughout Europe. Some of his most famous lines were in the poem "The Second Coming:"

The best lack all conviction, while the worst
Are full of passionate intensity.

And at the end of the same poem:

And what rough beast, its hour come round at last,
Slouches towards Bethlehem to be born?

Yeats also espoused some viewpoints that are doubtless more controversial today. He favored eugenics, saying "...we must limit the families of the unintelligent classes." He also saw some value in fascism, but more from a poetic than political viewpoint.

Yeats was born into a prosperous family in Dublin. Initially he studied portrait painting, but then decided he was more interested in writing. After some time in London he returned to Ireland for good in 1896. Early on he conceived a fascination with mysticism and the occult, an interest he retained throughout his life. He was also intrigued by Irish mythology, legends, and folk tales; many of his early works dealt with these subjects. His first poems were published in 1885 when he was just 20. In 1888 he came out with *Fairy & Folk Tales of the Irish Peasantry.* In 1891 he founded the Rhymers Club.

He helped establish the Irish Literary Theater and the famed Abbey Theater. As a major figure in Irish theater he both directed and wrote plays, with his works displaying a rich lyrical quality. In 1932 he founded the Irish Academy of Letters when he was 67. In his efforts, he encouraged and helped other Irish writers. He went on a lecture tour through the U.S. in 1920 and 1932. Shortly before he was 50 he began writing his autobiography and continued in spurts for the next couple of decades. Interest in the supernatural/occult and related subjects became a strong interest that was woven into his poetry.

Yeats also became involved in Irish politics, including a brief brush with the fascist Blue Shirts—a party mirroring to some extent the fascists in Germany and Italy—in Dublin during the 1930s. He exhibited some sympathy for right wing/authoritarian leaders such as Mussolini, mainly for establishing a semblance of order. After the creation of the Irish Free State in 1922 he became a senator in the new government (previously, in 1915, he had declined an offer of knighthood from Britain). He later received a honorary degree from Oxford University.

His last poem, "The Black Tower," written just a week before his death, involved Thoor Ballyle, an old Norman tower in poor condition that he restored as a summer home. Yeats died in Roquebrune-Cap-Martin in France. His remains were finally brought back to Ireland after World War II and he was buried at the Drumcliffe churchyard at Sligo with his ancestors. The epigraph on his gravestone, which came from one of his last poems, "Under Ben Bulben," read:

> *Cast a cold eye, on Life, on Death.*
> *Horseman, pass by!*

The Tower is now a tourist attraction. There is also a statue and a Yeats Memorial Building in Sligo containing various memorabilia of the writer. But his main testament remains in the power of his poetry.

"Education is not the filling of a pail, but the lighting of a fire."

"A pity beyond all telling is hid in the heart of love."

Ignace Jan Paderewski
1860–1941

"Before I was a genius I was a drudge."

A Renaissance style figure, Ignace Jan Paderewski made major contributions to the world and his native Poland as an outstanding musician and a significant statesman. As a musician—he was called a "poet of the piano"—he was a pianist and composer. As a statesman he helped create an independent Poland at the end of World War I (Poland had previously been carved up by Russia, Germany and Austria-Hungary), and then served as the country's prime minister and foreign minister and as its first delegate to the League of Nations. At the start of World War II, after Poland was invaded and occupied by Nazi Germany, he took over the reins of the Polish government-in-exile when he was already 80.

Paderewski was also a philanthropist, contributing generous sums from his concert earnings to many causes and charities.

Paderewski had an appendicitis operation when he was 69, but kept busy in his latter years on the musical and political fronts. One of his last projects was readying a new edition of the complete works of his fellow Polish musician, Frederic Chopin.

Paderewski was born in the village of Kurylouka in what is now the Ukraine. He studied at the Warsaw Musical Institute, and after graduating in 1878 taught there and also gave private lessons to augment a small income. He married young, but his wife died after a year, leaving him with a baby son.

Working hard, he became a piano virtuoso, and gave more than 1,500 concerts in his long career, drawing large crowds everywhere. He was the first pianist to give solo recitals, with the prior pattern being several artists on a program. He was the first to perform in an individual recital at the newly built Carnegie Hall in New York City.

He traveled through the United States in a private railroad car that had a piano. With his long golden/reddish hair he might have been the source for the expression "long-haired music." Such was his popularity that toys and candies, among other objects, were named after him. He received love letters and requests for autographed photos. Even some composers dedicated their creations to him. Other honors included honorary degrees and assorted medals. As a composer himself, he wrote a pair of operas, a symphony, and a violin and piano sonata.

The political phase of his life began several years before the first world war, when he began combining concerts with speeches calling for Polish independence. With the outbreak of the war in 1914 Polish-American organizations in the U.S. banded together and selected Paderewski as their leader. He helped form a volunteer force, which had camps on the American and Canadian sides of Niagara Falls. The soldiers at these camps finally saw action on the western front. As an honor, his name was listed on the rolls of each company, with "present" shouted when his name was called. He also succeeded in getting President Woodrow Wilson to support the creation of an independent Poland as part of the peace terms ending the conflict; playing the piano for the president and a group in the White House helped his cause.

After Poland was recognized internationally, Paderewski resigned as prime minister and minister of foreign affairs in 1919, unhappy with the political infighting and lack of support. He did represent Poland at an initial League of Nations conclave in Geneva, delivering a well-received speech while showing his mastery of several languages (he was fluent in seven). He gave this major address first in French and then repeated it in English.

Paderewski resumed his musical career in 1923, with refilling financial coffers a key reason. He continued performing until he retired from the concert stage in 1939. On his first U.S. tour he performed in 23 cities, earning around a half million dollars. He kept making benevolent contributions to various causes, including Jewish refugees from Nazi Germany and war orphans in Italy. In 1932, when he was 72, he turned over $50,000 from a Madison Square Garden event in New York to the benefit of unemployed American musicians. He also contributed a large sum to the American Legion for disabled veterans (becoming the first civilian foreigner to be made an honorary member), and of course to the Polish Victims Relief Fund.

His skill slipped, however, though he remained in demand. As a premier musician and elder statesman, he often consorted with world leaders, both elected officials and monarchs.

A foe of fascism, Paderewski refused to perform in Germany. In 1940, when back in the U.S. and already 80, he strongly advocated that the U.S. help Great Britain against the onslaught of Nazi Germany. In radio broadcasts, he urged America to "Stop Hitler before he masters the Atlantic!"

Though he lived at a villa in Morges, Switzerland, in 1913 he had also bought a ranch and some 2,600 acres near Paso Robles in Northern California, where grapes were planted; several of his wines won prizes. He named the ranch "Ignacio" after his patron saint.

Paderewski was very fond of the U.S. In his *The Paderewski Memoirs,* which came out in 1939, he wrote: "America, the country of my heart, my second home."

At the age of 76 he was a subject of a British film, *Moonlight Sonata.* A book, *Poland and Peace,* came out in 1933.

Paderewski was 79 and in poor health when Germany invaded Poland in 1939. Still he went to Paris to inaugurate the government-in-exile; he declined being named prime minister again. Subsequently he came to the U.S. to help the Polish cause. At a New York rally in June 1941 he collapsed from pneumonia and died several days later. His funeral mass at St. Patrick's Cathedral was attended by thousands, including luminaries from both the political and musical worlds. Paderewski's body was taken in a gun carriage pulled by eight horses to Penn Station in New York, and then by a special train to Washington D.C. By a special decree from Congress he was interred at Arlington National Cemetery, an honor to a non-American only bestowed once before in American history.

However, Paderewski's wish was to eventually be buried in Poland once his country was again free. His remains were finally re-interred in 1992, after the nation was no longer under Soviet domination, at a crypt in St. John's Cathedral in the Polish capital of Warsaw. But his heart is encased in a bronze sculpture at the Shrine of Czestochowa in Doylestown, PA.

SPLENDID SENIORS

Paderewski had strong views about the interaction of nationalism and music. He stated, "However great a man may be, his greatness is neither outside nor above the greatest of the nation."

Perhaps overly traditional, he found it difficult to accept some new forms of music, such as jazz, whose performers he once termed "the Bolsheviks of music."

Among many quotes:

"Art is the expression of the immortal part of man."

"I cannot imagine a genuinely happy home without music in it."

"Musical expression is never primarily national,
but is personal and individual rather.
It is so deep, so profound, that it goes beyond nationality
and gives voice to the most private feeling.
In music there is never heredity.
Each man is an individual."

"The culture of any country is gauged first
by its progress in art."

"If I don't practice for one day, I know it;
if I don't practice for two days, the critics know it;
if I don't practice for three days, the audience knows it."

Mohandas "Mahatma" Gandhi
1869–1948

"If my faith burns bright,
as I hope it will even if I stand alone,
I shall be alive in the grave,
and what is more, speaking from it."

One of the towering figures of the 20th century, Gandhi was a driving force in the ultimately successful struggle for Indian independence. Working well past his 65th birthday, he also strived tirelessly for Hindu-Moslem reconciliation in one nation in his senior years. His principles of civil disobedience and nonviolence to achieve political/social causes has been a model to other leaders including Martin Luther King, Jr. in the U.S. and Nelson Mandela in South Africa.

Gandhi was born in 1869 to a well-to-do Gujerati family in Porbandar. He was trained as a lawyer in London (where he finally found a vegetarian restaurant to serve the cuisine he was used to), receiving his degree in 1891. After some practice as an attorney back in India he accepted an offer to go Durban, South Africa on a case. He wound up staying in South Africa from 1893–1914, and fighting against the lack of civil liberties for Indians who were relegated to a lesser social status.

He conceived the practice of *satyagraha* ("hold fast to the truth," from the ancient Sanskrit *satya* for "truth" and *agraha* for "hold fast"), which parlayed the principles of civil disobedience and nonviolence into one creed; his rule became not to use violence to achieve justice even if violence was used against him. One of his favorite dictums was, "An eye for an eye makes the whole world blind."

Gandhi returned to India in 1915, when India was still part of the British empire, and joined the freedom movement, which led to his finally becoming president of the National Congress Party in 1923/24 and leader of the Indian Campaign for Home Rule. His style of living became ascetic, shunning western attire for traditional and simple Indian dress. He opined that Hindi should be the common language of

India and that he felt sinful when speaking English.

Utilizing the theme of nonviolent civil disobedience, he orchestrated major campaigns in the 1920s and 1930s—after his 65ᵗʰ birthday—which landed him in what he termed "His Majesty's Hotels" (jail). Overall, he spent seven years in jail (South Africa included), where he generally had more time to read and write. Fasts, protest marches, strikes, boycotts and other means were all put to use during the period between the world wars. To say he was a thorn in the side of the British, who were often baffled by his movement, would be an understatement.

One of the major events that drew worldwide attention and sympathy for the Indian cause was the famed 24-day "Salt March" of 1930. Indians had to pay a tax for salt and weren't allowed to produce their own salt from the sea. At age 61 Gandhi led a march of some 240 miles from Ahmedabad to the Arabian Sea to dramatize their plight. Beatings of Indians who didn't fight back helped bring even more support to Gandhi's efforts.

In 1931 he went to London for conferences on the Indian situation and its prospects for independence. The conference failed, with Gandhi hailed by some English notables and the public, but referred to as a "half-naked fakir" by Winston Churchill. While Churchill refused to see him, Gandhi, wearing his now familiar loincloth, did have tea at Buckingham Palace with King George V and Queen Mary. Questioned if his attire was sufficient for the occasion, Gandhi remarked that "The King had enough on for both of us."

In 1934, when he was 65, he formed the All-India Village Industries Association to further his program of self-reliance for Indians.

Gandhi chose to be celibate at 37 though married (he was married at 13 and had four children with Kasturba, his wife of 62 years). He was opposed to industrialization and favored self-sufficient villages sustained by cottage industries. He promoted agrarian reform. He also tried to foster Hindu-Moslem cooperation. In both of these objectives, especially the latter, he found little success. His attempt to improve the status of the "Untouchables," the lowest rung of people in the Hindu caste system, also proved to be too difficult to fully accomplish, though his work did lead to some improvement of their status. In 1933, he founded a paper, *Harijans* ("Children of God") to help the

Untouchables' deplorable situation.

He did help to get a limited measure of more home rule in 1935.

His leadership, marked by a simple demeanor and dress, led to him being known as the *Mahatma,* or "Great Soul," in the ancient Sanskrit language. He was also often called *Bapu* or "Little Father." Domestically, he was regarded as a holy man by India's downtrodden and many others as well. Internationally, he became a worldwide symbol of pacifism.

In 1943, under arrest for advocating non-cooperation with the British during World War II unless they agreed to Indian independence after the war, he was jailed and undertook a 21-day fast. The British released him before his sentence ran out.

His efforts helped to finally achieve independence for India in 1947. Gandhi was opposed to partition of India between Hindus and Moslems, but this separation—bloody and violent—still took place. He stressed that "India must see through both the Hindu eye and the Muslim eye, otherwise she is blind."

In another statement, often seen in signs at airports: "We must cease to be exclusive Hindus or Moslems or Sikhs, Parsis, Christians, or Jews. Whilst we may staunchly adhere to our respective faiths, we must be Indians first and Indians last."

Unfortunately, blindness reigned. At the age of 78 he began another fast-to-death in January 1948 to get the opposing Hindu and Moslem leaders to stop the internecine strife. Following a pledge five days later by both groups, he broke his fast. Unfortunately, he was assassinated just 12 days later by a Hindu extremist in New Delhi who opposed his policy of accord—short of approving partition—with the Moslem population and hoped his death would lead to India forcefully ending break-up of the country.

Worldwide laments, including a mourning period in the United Nations General Assembly, took place. A M.K. Gandhi Institute for Nonviolence was created after his death. Several memorials/statues and a major feature film commemorate his life.

Gandhi was nominated five times for the Nobel Prize, but never received the award. He produced many writings, including an autobiography that covered his life up to the age of 21. After that period, he felt his life was an open book.

Once, when asked what he thought about western civilization, Gandhi quipped, "I think it would be an excellent idea."

Among his many other quotes:

> *"Even as wisdom often comes from the mouths of babes, so does it often come from the mouths of old people."*

> *"As soon as we lose the moral basis, we cease to be religious."*

> *"An error does not become truth by reason of multiple propagation; nor does truth become error because nobody will see it."*

> *"True friendship is put to the test when one party disregards the obligation of friendship."*

> *"You must be the change you wish to see in the world."*

> *"There is a higher court than courts of justice and that is the court of conscience. It supersedes all other courts."*

> *"Healthy discontent is the prelude to progress."*

> *"Everyone who wills can hear the inner voice. It is within everyone."*

> *"Idealism sometimes causes pain, but a human being without idealism is like a brute."*

George Bernard Shaw
1856–1950

"Youth, which is forgiven everything,
forgives itself nothing;
age, which forgives itself everything,
is forgiven nothing."

During his long career, George Bernard Shaw—Irish author, playwright, and critic—wrote over 50 plays. He continued to write even in his 90s, and was working on a new play, *Why She Would Not,* when he died on Nov. 2, 1950 from complications after falling off a ladder while trimming a tree on his property at Ayot St. Laurence outside London. By his request his ashes were mixed with those of his wife, Charlotte, who had died seven years earlier. After his death became known in the U.S., all the lights on Broadway—including Times Square signs—were dimmed for five minutes as a tribute.

Among many honors, Shaw was the only person ever to receive both the Nobel Prize for Literature (1925) and an Academy Award (for his 1938 screenplay of *Pygmalion).* Shaw accepted the Nobel Prize, but refused the money portion in the belief that well-known writers didn't need the money; he donated the prize money to subsidize translating Swedish literature into English. In the same vein, Shaw declined a peerage for the House of Lords and even turned down the "Order of Merit," noting that the initials had come to stand for "Old Man"—a label he resisted even though he was in his 70s.

Among his works in his latter years, well after he was 75, were *Geneva* in 1938; *In Good King Charles' Golden Days* in 1939; and *Everybody's Political What's What* in 1944. His last full-length play, *Buoyant Billions,* was turned out when he was 92. He also wrote *Far Fetched Fables* and some of his memories in *Sixteen Self Sketches.*

Shaw was born in Dublin in 1856. His father's bouts with the bottle led Shaw to become a teetotaler for life. Eventually he became a vegetarian as well.

At the age of 15 he began work as a junior clerk for an estate office in Dublin. In 1876 he went to London to join his mother and sister there. He didn't return to his native Ireland for nearly 30 years. Self-taught to a large measure, Shaw spent a good deal of time in the British Museum absorbing world lore.

His literary career began with writing music and drama criticism for several London publications. He also wrote some novels, none successful. As to the vicissitudes of being a critic, he wrote, "To a professional critic (I have been one myself) theatre-going is the curse of Adam. The play is the evil he is paid to endure in the sweat of his brow; and the sooner it is over, the better."

His sympathies soon turned to societal problems, and he became involved with the Fabian Society, a socialist group that sought to redress social injustices. He served as the Society's executive director from 1885 through 1911. Shaw believed "property was theft," and wrote extensively on various issues such as the abolition of private property, women's rights, equality of income, and related subjects. He also lectured on socialism on street corners, and eventually became a popular orator.

Finally he turned to writing plays. Initially his plays might have been too ideological, but his works then began to incorporate a greater element of entertainment, which led to success and fame and even some considering him a "second Shakespeare" and the greatest English-speaking dramatist since Shakespeare. His major plays were *Man and Superman, Major Barbara, Pygmalion,* and *John Bull's Other Island.*

When some of his plays were later published, a distinctive aspect of these books were extensive essays on the issues involved that were longer than the plays themselves. Essentially Shaw focused more on ideas than on characters in his plays, though he was fascinated by the great men of history. He also was keen on having his plays read as well as produced, and later categorized them as "Plays Unpleasant" and "Plays Pleasant."

He married Charlotte Payne-Townsend, an Irish woman of independent means, in 1898, and they were together for the rest of her life. He carried on an intense correspondence with two famed actresses, Stella Campbell (who starred in *Pygmalion)* and Ellen Terry. These letters, sort of an epistolary love affair (his relationships with women were considered to be on the platonic side), were later both publicized and dramatized.

In the 1930s Shaw, following the socialism impetus, visited Russia. He was impressed, and approved of Stalin and the Soviet Union as getting good things done "much more promptly than parliaments." He also found initial praise for both Mussolini and Hitler. The extent to which he later came to understand the true nature and perils of dictators and a totalitarian state isn't clear.

One of his projects for many years, continued in his later years, was a drive to revamp the English alphabet along phonetic lines. Sometimes dubbed the "Shavian alphabet," this effort involved an alphabet with 40 characters that he felt would make it easier to spell and write English. Between the two World Wars he served as chairman of the British Broadcasting Company's committee for spoken English. He even left money for the alphabet project, which never came to fruition, in his will. Instead his money was given to the Irish National Gallery of Art, the Royal Academy of Art, and the British Museum.

Among his works written after 65 was *Saint Joan* (1924), considered his masterpiece. Other works during this latter stage of his life were *The Intelligent Woman's Guide to Socialism* in 1928, *The Apple Cart* in 1929, *Too Good to be True* in 1932, *American Boobs* in 1933, *Sixteen Self Sketches* in 1948, and *Far Fetched Fables* in 1950. Two other important plays were *Heartbreak House* in 1919 and *Back To Methuselah* in 1921, the year he turned 65.

Films generated by Shaw's plays include two versions of *Pygmalion* (one a musical version retitled *My Fair Lady*); *Saint Joan*, 1927; *How He Lied to Her Husband,* 1931; *Arms and the Man,* 1932; and *Major Barbara,* 1941. Initially he was somewhat suspicious of the new medium of film, fearful of losing control of his plays and having scenes and dialogue changed; but eventually he even wrote new scenes for the movies himself.

Shaw's drama pieces were collected in *Our Theatre in the Nineties,* with his music reviews in *Shaw's Music.*

A George Bernard Shaw Society in New York continues to commemorate his work and impact on western culture.

Famed for his ironic humor, often referred to as "Shavian wit," here are some of his more notable quotes:

"England and America are two countries divided by the same language."

"Christianity might be a good thing if anyone ever tried it."

"Americans adore me and will go on adoring me until I say something nice about them."

"Life does not cease to be funny when people die anymore than it ceases to be serious when people laugh."

"Liberty means responsibility; that's why most men dread it."

"Martyrdom is the only way a person can become famous without ability."

"Democracy is a device that insures we will be governed no better than we deserve."

"Dancing is a perpendicular expression of a horizontal desire."

"Youth is a wonderful thing. What a shame to waste it on children."

"A fashion is nothing but an induced epidemic."

"No diet will remove the fat from your body because the brain is entirely fat. Without a brain, you might look good, but all you could do is run for public office."

George Santayana
1863–1952

"Those who cannot remember the past are condemned to repeat it."

This is probably the most famous and most quoted aphorism delivered by George Santayana, a philosopher, writer and cultural critic who was a key personality in the period often referred to as "classical American philosophy."

Santayana's sense of philosophy contained elements of naturalism with a strong dose of skepticism. He explored spirituality without being overly religious, and celebrated the world of imagination without pedantry. He wrote: "...cultivate imagination, love it, give it endless forms, but do not let it deceive you. Enjoy the world, travel about it, and learn its ways, but do not let it hold you. To possess things and persons in idea is the only pure good to be got out of them; to possess them physically or legally is a burden and a snare."

Another of his dictums was: "There are three traps that strangle philosophy: the Church, the marriage-bed, and the professor's chair." Santayana, it should be added, never married.

Santayana was born in Madrid, Spain in 1863. His family moved to Boston when he was nine and spoke Spanish for the most part at home. While he wrote in English, Santayana retained his Spanish citizenship throughout his life. His Spanish and European heritage probably contributed to his being able to assess American culture so keenly.

After earning his undergraduate degree from Harvard in 1899 he became a professor at that university, teaching philosophy from 1889 to 1912. However, he tired of the constraints of academic life and what he described as the "thistles of trivial and narrow scholarship." He planned an early retirement in which he could employ his own imagination and write at will. Subsequently he left for Europe when nearly

50 and never returned to the U.S.

A substantial sum left to him by his mother helped financially. As a scholar gypsy he roamed a bit in Europe before settling in Rome as his base, where he continued his prolific output of criticism and other writings.

One of his best known works, *The Last Puritan,* a memoir-style novel that was a best seller, came out in 1935 when he was 72. The book received a nomination for a Pulitzer Prize. Other key works after he was 65 include his three-volume autobiography, *Persons and Places,* (1944–1953), *The Middle Span* (1945), *The Idea of Christ in the Gospels* (1946), and *Dominations & Powers* (1951). *My Host, the World* was published posthumously in 1953.

The Realms of Being, a great opus, appeared in four volumes spread between 1927 and 1940. Over 3,000 of his letters to over 350 people have been collected in *The Letters of George Santayana.*

Santayana first achieved fame with publication of his *The Sense of Beauty* in 1896. However, his masterpiece is considered to be the five-volume *The Life of Reason: Phases of Human Progress,* which was published during 1905–06. Other significant works include *Interpretation of Poetry & Religion* in 1900, *Character & Opinion in the United States* in 1920, and *Scepticism & Animal Faith* in 1923.

Santayana wrote a great deal about religion and its role in life, believing in the spirituality of religion more than the dogma of Catholicism, his faith. Religions, Santayana opined, are "the great fairy-tales of the conscience." Yet he also said, "Religion in its humility restores man to his only dignity, the courage to live by grace."

In another comment on the close relationship between religion and poetry, he wrote, "Poetry is called religion when it intervenes in life; and religion, when it merely supervenes upon life, is seen to be nothing but poetry."

Initially he approved of the order that Mussolini brought to Italy, but then he realized *Il Duce* was a dictator. Santayana attempted to leave Italy for neutral Switzerland with war clouds descending, but he was prevented on the grounds that he lacked the correct papers. Back in Rome, he entered a Catholic hospital/clinic (explaining he was a non-practicing Catholic) that often cared for distinguished guests in an assisted-living arrangement. He lived there in relative seclusion but failing health (including hearing problems), while continuing to write, for the last 11 years of his life. He passed away in 1952, concerned that the priests might be "standing around waiting for a last-minute conversion."

Santayana had requested that he be buried in unconsecrated ground, which was consistent with his naturalistic philosophy. But this posed a problem, as the only such site available in Rome was said to be for criminals. Santayana was still a Spaniard, and the Spanish Consulate in Rome refused to let him be buried at such a questionable site. Instead, they created a little Spanish section at the Campo Verano cemetery that turned into a memorial for Santayana. Lines from his poem "The Poet's Testament" were read at his graveside:

> I give back to the earth what the earth gave,
> All to the furrow, nothing to the grave.
> The candle's out, the spirit's vigil spent,
> Sight may not follow where the vision went.

Some other of Santayana's sayings:

> "Fanaticism consists in redoubling your effort
> when you have forgotten your aim."

> "The moment we turn the magic of the moment into a maxim,
> we have clouded the sky."

> "Scepticism is the chastity of the intellect,
> and it is shameful to surrender it too soon
> or to the first comer."

> "Sanity is a madness put to good use, waking life is a dream controlled."

> "Nothing so much enhances a good as to make sacrifices for it."

> "…when men and women argue it is only in their conclusions;
> their reasons are always different."

> "Fun is a good thing, but only when it spoils nothing better."

> "History is a pack of lies about events that never happened
> told by people who weren't there."

Splendid Seniors

"The wisest mind has something yet to learn."

"Life as it flows is so much time wasted, and nothing can ever be recovered or truly possessed save under the form of eternity, which is also the form of art."

"…only the dead have seen the end of war."

"Love makes us all poets, and the approach of death should make us philosophers."

Albert Einstein
1879–1955

*"There are only two ways
to live your life.*
One is as though nothing is a miracle.
The other is as though everything is a miracle."

One of the greatest scientists of any age, and the most famous theoretical physicist in history, Einstein changed the way we perceived our universe with his theory of relativity, radically changing our notion of time and space. His $E=mc^2$, the relationship between energy, mass and the speed of light, became the most famous equation in the world.

Einstein proved, mathematically, that gravitational effects are due to the curvature of space rather than to physical forces. He won the Nobel Prize in 1921 when he was 42 (after being rejected several times).

His theories played a role in the development of atomic energy. In a letter to President Roosevelt in 1939, he stressed the importance of beating Nazi Germany to the military use of atomic energy. His opinion was a factor in the later formation of the Manhattan Project, in which the U.S. created the first atomic bomb.

However, subsequently he wrote: "I do not consider myself the father of the release of atomic energy. My part in it was quite indirect. I did not, in fact, foresee that it would be released in my time. I believed only that it was theoretically possible."

With news that an atomic bomb had destroyed much of Hiroshima, Einstein was greatly saddened and muttered *"Vey iz mir"*—"Woe is me."

In another statement about his missive to Roosevelt, he said, "I think I have made one mistake in my life, to have signed that letter. But perhaps I may be excused because we were all afraid the Germans would be getting the atom bomb." Later, he also warned that not much of civilization would survive an atomic war.

Einstein, who knew the Germans all too well, had warned Winston Churchill early in the 1930s that Germany was re-arming for eventual war.

His advancing age and deteriorating health didn't stop him from working. When he was already past 65, Einstein wrote to an 80-year-old friend that they aged differently than others. "What I mean is that we never cease to stand like curious children before the great Mystery into which we are born."

While much praised and honored—he was called a "Jewish saint" and "the greatest Jew since Jesus"—Einstein was also investigated by the FBI for supposed Communist ties. His huge file was finally closed without ever having amounted to anything other than another hallmark of the McCarthy era.

Though born as a Jew, Einstein admitted that "I never felt myself part of the Jewish race till late in life, when I saw and felt the sting of anti-Semitism, particularly in Germany."

Born in Ulm, Germany in 1879, his mother, Pauline, thought he was deformed, as his head was large and oddly shaped. There was nothing wrong with him, though he did have an unusually large head. Einstein was not particularly bright in elementary school, and later said he was slow in learning to talk because he was "waiting" until he could deliver fully formed sentences. Still, he was at the top of classes in both math and Latin. When he was five his father gave him a compass, which so excited him that he "trembled and grew cold."

He studied in Germany and Switzerland. He loathed German militarism, and was aghast at the plunge toward World War I. His return to Berlin from Switzerland led him "to discover for the first time he was a Jew."

Einstein tried to reconcile the world of science and religion, though he was hardly religious in the sense of the tenets of Judaism. This ongoing effort may have led him to resist the causality put forward by the proponents of quantum mechanics—how particles of the universe interact—and the "uncertainty principle." Einstein famously said, "God doesn't play dice with the universe."

With the advent of the Nazis Einstein came to the U.S. Though world-famous, his theories had been branded as a "Jewish fraud" and "Jewish science" by the Nazis. Though he never met Adolf Hitler, he usually responded when asked about the Fuhrer, "No, but I have seen his photographs, and they are sufficient."

In 1933 he accepted a position as a professor at the Institute of Advanced Studies at Princeton, N.J. which he described in this fashion: "Princeton is a wonderful piece of earth, and at the same time an exceedingly amusing ceremonial backwater of tiny spindle-shanked demigods." In 1940 he became an American citizen (while retaining his Swiss citizenship). He spent the rest of his life in America. During World War II he served as a consultant with the U.S. Navy on proposals for new weapons and critiques of those on the drawing boards. He retired in 1945 and spent the last 30 years in pursuit of a theory that could unify all of physics.

He suffered a setback in 1936 when his wife, Elsa, died, but he coped through work. "But as long as I am able to work I must not and will not complain, because work is the only thing which gives substance to life."

Einstein had mixed but somewhat optimistic feelings over the future betterments of society that might come from the advancements of technology and scientific discoveries. In a time capsule sealed at the 1939 World's Fair, he opined: "...the production and distribution of commodities is entirely unorganized so that everybody must live in fear of being eliminated from the economic cycle. Furthermore, people living in different countries kill each other at irregular time intervals, so that also for this reason anyone who thinks about the future must live in fear and terror. I trust that posterity will read these statements with a feeling of proud and justified supremacy."

In 1946 he became president of the Emergency Committee of Atomic Scientists. Einstein became renowned as a pacifist, describing himself as being opposed to the "use of" force under any circumstances except when confronted by an enemy who pursues the destruction of life as an end in itself." In addition, he said, "As long as armies exist, any serious conflict will lead to war. A pacifism which does not actively fight against the armament of nations is and must remain impotent." He favored the creation of a world government, writing that "as long as sovereign states continue to have separate armaments and armaments secrets, new world wars will be inevitable."

In 1949 his *Autobiographical Notes* was published, but this tome covers how he developed his theories and not his personal life. A year later, another book, *Out of My Later Years,* was published.

A supporter of the state of Israel, he still declined an offer of the presidency of the fledgling nation in 1952.

In his personal life, which was greatly overshadowed by his public persona, he was not considered to be a particularly ideal husband and father; he was also said to have fathered an illegitimate child among some paramours. One of his apropos comments: "There is far too great a disproportion between what one is and what others think one is." On marriage, he said, "Marriage is the unsuccessful attempt to make something lasting out of an incident."

While science was his field, Einstein was also considered a proficient violinist.

As sickness overcame him, he wrote that death was "a debt one eventually pays," and the prolongation of life artificially was not to his taste. He died on April 18, 1955.

Before his remains were cremated, several oddities occurred. His eyeballs reportedly came into the keeping of an ophthalmologist friend who placed them in a safety deposit box. Even stranger, the pathologist who did the autopsy took possession of Einstein's brain, which was subsequently separated into more than 200 parts for possible study. Eventually, the remnants of Einstein's much-traveled brain were returned in 1996 to Princeton Hospital, site of the original autopsy.

One signal honor, though it came posthumously, was having a man-made element, "einsteinium," named after him.

Einstein was modest in his way, once stating,

He who finds a thought that lets us penetrate even a little deeper into the eternal mystery of nature has been granted great grace. He who, in addition, experiences the recognition, sympathy, and help of the best minds of his time, has been given almost more happiness than a man can bear.

Some of his other comments were:

"A clever person solves problems. A wise person avoids it."

*"Insanity is doing the same thing over and over—
and expecting different results."*

"The difference between genius and stupidity is that genius has its limits."

"As far as the laws of mathematics refer to reality, they are not certain; and as far as they are certain, they do not refer to reality."

"Education is what remains after one has forgotten everything he learned in school."

"I know not with what weapons World War III will be fought, but World War IV will be fought with sticks and stones."

Thomas Mann
1875–1955

"No man remains quite what he was
when he recognizes himself."

One of the greatest writers of the 20th century, Thomas Mann received the Nobel Prize for literature in 1929 for his novel *Buddenbrooks,* which traced the fortunes of a German family over four generations, mostly from affluence to decadence.

His output continued well past his 65th birthday, including such major works as *Dr. Faustus,* a modern version of the Faust legend, which came out in 1948 when he was 73. Other books included *The Transposed Heads* in 1940 and *The Holy Sinner* in 1951. Mann also kept working on an unfinished novel, *Confessions of Felix Krull, Confidence Man.*

Many of his writings centered around the tensions between the artist and society, and the psychology of the creative artist. His diaries, unsealed in 1975, revealed his own troubled homosexual concerns. His 1912 novella, *Death in Venice,* reflects the latter subject in moving and telling fashion. The novella was also made into a movie.

Mann was born in Lubeck, Germany in 1875. He lived in Munich for many years. His first story, "Fallen," appeared in 1894, followed by a collection of short stories in 1898. But it was the publication of *Buddenbrooks* in 1901 that catapulted him to fame and considerable wealth by the time he was 25.

Despite his worries over his sexual identity, he married his wife, Katia—who came from a Jewish family—in 1905. They had six children, who all became writers.

Initially Mann favored Germany and the monarchy at the outset of the first World War, but his views changed as the war progressed badly for Germany and his viewpoint became more attuned to democratic values. His reappraisal of the European political/social scene led to another major novel, *The Magic Mountain.* He also turned out essays, as well as speeches, about the German economic crisis and the rise of fascism. In due course he became unpopular in Germany, with the Nazis launching a campaign of abuse against him. His German citizenship was revoked in 1936, retroactive to 1933, and some honorary doctorates from German universities were also cancelled. (But in the U.S. Mann, along with Albert Einstein, received honorary doctorates from Harvard in 1935.)

Before Hitler took over Germany formally in 1933 as chancellor, Mann and his family emigrated to Kilchberg, near Zurich, in Switzerland, However, he left some diaries at his Munich home that he felt could be ruinous to his reputation (he had burned some diaries much earlier, and more would be destroyed later in the U.S.). He went to the U.S. in 1938 and taught at Princeton University in New Jersey for two years. In 1940 he moved to the Pacific Palisades section of Los Angeles. He received his American citizenship in 1944, though culturally he retained some semblance of European formality (especially in relation to the casualness of Los Angeles), even to the extent of donning a suit and tie simply to walk his dog.

During the second World War he published articles and made broadcast speeches on behalf of the Allied forces while still trying to represent what was good in German culture. President Roosevelt, with whom he once had dinner, even considered giving Mann a top position in handling postwar Germany.

Earlier, Mann began a quartet of books about the biblical character Joseph, with the group including *The Tales of Joseph,* 1933; *The Young Joseph,* 1934; *Joseph in Egypt,* 1936, and *Joseph the Provider,* 1943. While these books were begun in Munich in 1925, when he was 50, they were completed in Pacific Palisades, California in 1943, when he was over 70.

Mann also kept writing essays, including "On Myself" (1940), which covered the breakdown of civilization, and the collection *Essays of Three Decades* (1947), which dealt with various literary matters. His major political essays and speeches were published in *Order of the Day* in 1942. He endured a lung cancer operation in 1946, and removal of some ribs, while continuing work on his *Dr. Faustus.* In the "Goethe

Year" of 1949 he gave various lectures and wrote the essay "Goethe and Democracy."

Mann ran into difficulties with the much criticized hearings held by Senator Joseph McCarthy, as he was accused of being "left wing" and a "fellow traveler." Magazines dubbed his political position the "Way of the Dupe." Some suspicion had arisen after he visited East Germany and his alleged but not necessarily accurately reported involvements with liberal causes and groups. Mann fought back with the comment, "I am neither a dupe nor a fellow traveler and by no means an admirer of the quite malicious present phase of the Russian revolution." But he was also somewhat dubious about the political trends in the West.

Consequently disappointed in the political climate (hardly an admirer of Richard Nixon, he termed the politician's famous "Checkers" speech "television comedy"), he left the United States in 1952 and returned to Switzerland, where he lived again near Zurich. "My home is in the works I carry with me," he wrote.

Despite his advanced age and declining health (lung cancer had been diagnosed in 1946 and dental problems forced the pulling of all his teeth a year earlier), he continued to write daily, including essays and articles about events in both West and East Germany. When he was 75 he wrote an essay, "Michelangelo's Erotic Poetry." His last major piece was the 80-page "Essay on Friedrich Schiller" in 1954 when nearly 80.

Honors poured in on his 80th birthday, extolling his role as one of the elder statesmen of literature. He died in 1955.

Among his many quotes of note:

> *"War is only a cowardly escape from the problems of peace."*

> *"A man's dying is more the survivors' affair than his own."*

> *"If you are possessed by an idea, you find it expressed everywhere; you even smell it."*

> *"The only religious way to think of death is as part and parcel of life."*

> *"All interest in diseases and death is only another expression of interest in life."*

> *"A great truth is a truth whose opposite is also a great truth."*

JACK ADLER

"It is love, not reason, that is stronger than death."

"Speech is civilization itself. The word, even the most contradictory word, preserves contact—it is silence which isolates."

From *The Magic Mountain:*

"A man lives not only his personal life, as an individual, but also, consciously or unconsciously, the life of his epoch and his contemporaries."

Arturo Toscanini
1867–1957

"If you want to please the critics,
don't play too loud, too soft, too fast, too slow."

In his early school years in Parma, Italy, Toscanini was called "Genius" by some friends due to his prodigious memory; but he was also nicknamed "Scissors" because of his tendency to be critical. In his later years, after he had become of the most renowned conductors in the world, he was dubbed "The Maestro." Other encomiums included being called "the greatest conductor of his time" and "the greatest musical interpreter who ever lived." What is certain is that Toscanini helped popularize classical music to the American people over a very long and active performing career.

In 1937, at the age of 69, after a 50-year career that would have made most persons content to savor the joys of retirement, Toscanini opted to continue working as a conductor. He accepted an offer from NBC and became conductor of the new NBC Philharmonic Orchestra. For 17 years he conducted weekly broadcasts of concerts on radio that greatly helped to present classical music to a wide audience. He also made recordings. Overall, some 480 symphonic works by 175 composers were broadcast during this period.

Toscanini's influence still permeates the musical world. He was justly famed both for his vitriolic temper and for demanding more musical skill from orchestra members than other conductors of his day and before. However, even musicians who experienced one of his tirades felt that working with Toscanini was a milestone in their own careers. His style of conducting to some extent shook the musical world with the way he shaped the composers' scores, enhancing their interpretation while still remaining true to the works. One of his more famous quips was about Beethoven's Symphony #3 *(Eroica):* "To some it is Napoleon, to some it's a philosophical struggle, to me it is *allegro con brio.*"

The great conductor was born in the northern Italian city of Parma in 1867. He showed early promise while studying the cello. His conducting career began in 1886 in Rio de Janeiro, during a tour, when he was suddenly called upon to take over at a concert featuring *Aida.* His phenomenal memory served him well, and his career blossomed and lasted 68 years. For half of those years, 1920–1954, he was also a recording artist.

Toscanini became principal conductor of the famed La Scala in Milan in 1898. He made his American debut in 1908, and performed with the Metropolitan Opera until 1915. Acclaim came quickly. During World War I he was back in Italy and even went to the front with a military band. In 1926 he began an association with the New York Philharmonic Orchestra that lasted to 1935.

In 1930 he was the first non-German to conduct at the Bayreuth Festival. However, with the advent of Hitler and fascism in Germany, he refused to perform again at Bayreuth in 1933, when he was already 66, in protest over the persecution of Jews. He even sent Hitler a telegram to this effect. The Fuhrer's response was to ban further sales of Toscanini's recordings.

In his native Italy, after initial support of Mussolini, Toscanini became disillusioned with the Italian dictator's brand of fascism. He showed his opposition by refusing to perform the fascist anthem at concerts. This led to his being attacked by fascist thugs.

At his own expense Toscanini went to Palestine in 1936 to conduct a new orchestra composed of Jewish refugees. The orchestra subsequently became the Israel Philharmonic. Performances were held in Jerusalem, Haifa and Tel Aviv. In 1938, when Italy passed a series of racial laws, Toscanini returned to Palestine—despite threats to his safety—for more concerts.

In the 1930s he also performed in other European capitals such as Paris, Vienna and Stockholm. He helped launch a new Lucerne Festival in the Swiss city. When Austria was absorbed by Nazi Germany he withdrew from performing at the Salzburg Festival. During World War II he performed benefit concerts for the War Orphan Committee, Infantile Paralysis Fund and Child Welfare League.

With the fall of Mussolini and the end of World War II, he sought to help his native country reach stability. "I am an old artist who had been among the first to denounce fascism to the world. I feel and believe that I can act as interpreter of the soul of the Italian people—these people whose voice has been choked for 20 years, but, thanks to God, just now is shouting for peace and liberty."

After World War II Toscanini returned to Italy from the U.S. to help La Scala, which had been damaged by bombs, resume as a world-class institution. Thereafter, he returned to Europe for some time every year. He was also appointed a senator for life by a grateful Italian government.

Toscanini performed with the NBC Symphony from 1937 through 1954, with performances on television starting in 1948.

In 1951, at the age of 84, Toscanini had a minor stroke while out on his exercise bicycle. Still, he kept working. But his extraordinary memory failed him at last during a rehearsal, and he decided to retire. His final concert was on April 4, 1954. Toscanini always described himself as an "honest musician," and when a respectful admirer addressed him afterward as "Maestro," he poignantly answered, "Do not call me Maestro. I am no longer *maestro.*"

Toscanini suffered a final stroke on January 1, 1957 and died on January 16 that year. He received what was virtually a state funeral, with many eulogies. His burial was in a family tomb in Milan.

Among his comments (some might say outbursts):

"God tells me how the music should sound, but you stand in the way."

"Can't you read? The score demands 'con amore' and what are you doing? You are playing it like married men."

"After I die, I shall return to earth as a gatekeeper of a bordello and I won't let any of you—not a one of you—enter."

"When I was young, I kissed my first woman, and smoked my first cigarette on the same day. I have never had time for tobacco since."

Frank Lloyd Wright
1867–1959

"There is nothing more uncommon
than common sense."

One of the greatest and most innovative architects of the 20th century, especially in his own estimation, as he was not known for his modesty, Wright never retired, continuing to work until his death shortly before the age of 92. Overall he designed over a thousand structures, with more than 400 built. Many still stand as testimonials to his architectural innovations. With his career spanning more than seven decades, Wright managed to design many of his works during the last 16 years of his life while his health was declining (ear problems among other ailments).

On his 80th birthday he declared, "A creative life is a young one. But what makes you think that 80 is old?"

Among the famous buildings that he worked on after he was 75 were the S.C. Johnson Research Tower in Racine, Wisconsin; the V.C. Morris Gift Shop in San Francisco; the Unitarian Church, Madison, Wisconsin; and the Marin County Civic Center, San Rafael, California.

Two of his most famous buildings, Fallingwater (with parts of the house cantilevered over a waterfall) at Bear Run, Pennsylvania and the Johnson Wax Headquarters in Racine, Wisconsin were designed in 1936 when he was already 69. Fallingwater was selected as the "Building of the Century" in 2000 by the American Institute of Architects. The Johnson Wax Administration Building in Racine was completed in 1939 when he was 72. Three other famous buildings, built after World War II when he was in his 70s, were the Price Tower in Bartleville, Oklahoma, the Guggenheim Museum in New York City, and the Marin County Civic Center.

Wright, noted for his pioneering work in architecture, was the first American architect to utilize innovative "open space" designs in the interior space of residential homes. His reduction of more traditional closed-space rooms (termed "Victorian boxes" by some), which often meant taking out walls between rooms, had a major impact on architecture. "The space within a building is the reality of the building," Wright opined. "A building is not just a place to be. It is a way to be."

He came up with what was called the "Prairie" type of architecture, featuring low-pitched roofs, earthy colors and low horizontal lines that blended into the landscape. He espoused what was termed "organic architecture," with use of more unadorned natural materials, describing this style as one that "creates according to the nature of man and his circumstances as they change." In effect, he disliked houses and rooms that resembled boxes too much and sought architecture that provided natural, free flowing links between people and their environment.

His most famous examples of the "Prairie" style are in Chicago and its suburbs, including the Willis, Coonley and Robie houses, all erected in the 1900–1909 period.

Wright's work was praised in Europe as early as pre-World War I, but recognition from some quarters came later in the U.S. It wasn't until 1949, for example, that the American Institute of Architects gave him an award.

Wright went against one of the major international architectural trends of the period, which favored greater utilitarian use of space and building materials including reinforced concrete. "I find myself a man without a country, architecturally speaking, at the present time," he said in 1932. However, he insisted he wouldn't alter his own principles. Others derided him as "Frank Wright Wrong" and the "greatest architect of the 19th century."

In 1932, when he suffered from an inner ear problem among other ailments, he also began training young architects in paid-for fellowships at his famed Taliesin West ("shining brow" in Welsh) school near Scottsdale, Arizona, a successor to the initial Taliesin in Wisconsin. The "school" helped revive his flagging finances, which had been hurt by his marital woes (he had been accused of violating the Mann Act—transporting a woman across state lines for illegal sexual purposes—among other divorce-related problems) and the Crash of 1929.

As Wright's reputation picked up he became a pundit on architecture as well as other subjects. He received many honors for his work, including his likeness on a two-cent stamp and the cover of *Time* magazine's Jan. 17, 1938 issue.

Perhaps on the naïve side, he was impressed with the Soviet Union—other than by its architecture—in a 1937 trip when he was 70. His belief in pacifism, and sympathy shown to pre-World War II Germany and Japan, led the FBI to push for but fail to prosecute Wright on a charge of sedition. After the war he was then accused of Communist leanings due to his comments for disarmament and world peace. He was also cited by the House Un-American Activities Committee in 1951 for affiliation with alleged Communist-front organizations. He was in good company with Albert Einstein and Thomas Mann, among other luminaries, also under suspicion.

Still architecturally innovative, Wright developed a style of low-cost, single-story homes which he called "Usonian" (combining "useful" and "U.S.") The prototypes for this brand were the First Usonian Meeting House, which arose in Madison, Wisconsin in the 1947–50 period, and the Jacobs house near Madison.

Wright was born in Richland Center in Wisconsin on June 8, 1867. In 1887 he became a draftsman at a Chicago architectural firm co-run by famed designer Louis Sullivan. He became greatly influenced by the dictum he learned there that "form follows function." During this period he designed, on his own, several houses with low sheltered roof lines, foretelling some of his future work. Taking on too many freelance assignments led to his being let go. He started his own firm in 1893.

One of his major projects was the design of the Imperial Hotel in Tokyo, a six-year project, 1916–1922. The hotel survived the disastrous 1923 earthquake in Tokyo, with Wright's support and safety features (use of floating foundations that moved rather than being solidly connected to the ground) said to be a major factor. Another major structure he helped design was the Arizona Biltmore Hotel in Phoenix in 1927.

Many of his books and lectures were published and given after he was 65. These include:

An Organic Architecture, 1939; *On Architecture,* 1941; *When Democracy Builds,* 1945; *Genius & the Mobocracy,* 1949; *The Future of Architecture,* 1953; *An American Architecture,* 1955; and *A Testament,* 1957. His *An Autobiography* came out in 1943 (though written much earlier), along with *The Disappearing City,* in which he advocated more single-family houses and less urban congestion. *Modern Architecture,* based on university lectures, was published in 1931.

Wright had the dubious distinction of being the partial model for the major character, an iconoclastic architect, in the best-selling 1943 novel (and subsequent film) *The Fountainhead.* The author, Ayn Rand, had spent time with Wright. Initially, Wright was unhappy with the literary/cinematic association, terming it an "abusive caricature," but later indicated he could see some compatibility with the character.

Wright died in 1959. The last of his three wives, Olgivanna—whom he married in 1928 when he was 61 and she was more than 30 years younger—ran Taliesin until she died in 1985. He had gone through a difficult period disentangling from his first and second wives, which damaged his financial situation as well as reputation. Overall, he had seven children. The epitaph at his grave reads: "Love of an idea is the love of God."

Among the many quotes attributed to Wright, especially after his acclaim as an "architectural hero" by the media, were:

"The mother art is architecture. Without an architecture of our own, we have no soul of our own civilization."

"The artist himself, of course, is of his time or he is not an artist. He is the prophet of his time and of his day; he is the seeing-eye of his people."

"The longer I live, the more beautiful life becomes."

"Old as man's moral life is this urge to grow."

"I believe in God, only I spell it nature."

"The physician can bury his mistakes, but the architect can only advise his client to plant vines."

"Space is the breath of art."

JACK ADLER

"An idea is salvation by imagination."

"TV is chewing gum for the eyes."

"The heart is the chief feature of a functioning mind,"

"If it keeps up, man will atrophy all his limbs but the push-button finger."

"The truth is more important than the facts."

As an acerbic reference to Southern California:

"It is as if you tipped the United States up so all the commonplace people slid down there into Southern California."

Also on the lighter side, he said of Marilyn Monroe:

"I think Ms. Monroe's architecture is extremely good architecture."

Grandma Moses
1860–1961

"If I didn't start painting,
I would have raised chickens.
I could still do it now."

So wrote Anna Mary Robertson, known as "Grandma Moses," in her 1952 autobiography, *My Life's History*, when she was 92. Representing one of the most remarkable stories of late-life achievement in the annals of mankind, she has been a shining example to many seniors for her ability to start a new career, and a creative one, when she was well beyond 65 and not in the best of health. And as a woman, she was the first distaff artist to become an international celebrity.

Wife of a farmer in upstate New York, she only started painting as a major part of her life at the age of 78, when the rigors of old age had already set in. Despite creakier hand movements and less sharpness of vision, she continued painting for the rest of her life. Living over 100 years, she created some 2,000 works of art.

"I never know how I'm going to paint until I start in; something tells me what to go right on and do." She added that she "painted for pleasure, to keep busy and to pass the time away…"

Painting primarily from memory, often of the many routine tasks and chores of farm life, and exhibiting a natural talent for color and composition, she described nostalgic scenes of rural Americana that she called "old-timey" farm life. Paintings titles included *Catching the Thanksgiving Turkey, Out for the Christmas Trees, Over the River to Grandma's House*, and *Sugaring-Off in the Maple Orchard*. Some works had nursery-rhyme themes like *Little Boy Blue* and *Mary and Little Lamb*.

As late as 1960, when she was 99, Grandma Moses took on an assignment from Random House to illustrate the famous poem *The Night Before Christmas*. She completed her last illustration after her

100th birthday. She also produced 25 paintings after her 100th birthday, showing a remarkable ability to continue her art output as well as an inimitable work ethic.

In her autobiography Grandma Moses wrote, "I look back on my life like a good day's work; it was done and I feel satisfied with it. I was happy and contented. I knew nothing better and made the best out of what life offered and life is what we make it, always has been, always will be."

Grandma Moses had little formal education during her childhood. Leaving her parents' farm at Greenwich, New York, she labored as a hired girl until marrying Thomas Moses in 1887. After a stint of farming in Virginia, they moved to a farm at Eagle Bridge in New York near her birthplace. She gave birth to 10 children between 1887 and 1905, with just half surviving infancy. After her husband's death in 1927 she continued to operate the farm until moving to a sick daughter's home in Bennington, Vermont in 1936 to help care for her and her children. She later returned to upstate New York, where she purchased a farm.

Turning to painting after arthritis made threading and handling a needle too difficult for her to continue to create worsted embroidery pictures, she used illustrated postcards and Currier & Ives prints as models. But as her self-taught skills matured, she started to paint scenes she retained from her childhood and life's experiences, still coping stoically with the difficulties of arthritis as well as other enfeeblements of advancing age.

Initially, her first paintings—presented at county fairs and church sales—were either sold for little money or just given away. As chance would have it, a bunch of her paintings on display in a drugstore window in Hoosick Falls, New York in 1939 drew the attention of an art collector who was sufficiently impressed to subsequently track her down to her farm. At her farm the collector was shown more of her work, and ultimately purchased several of her paintings. Three of those paintings were then exhibited later that year at the Museum of Modern Art in New York City in an exhibit called "Contemporary Unknown American Painters."

Her work was well received, and her career as a major artist blossomed. A one-woman show involving 35 paintings was held in 1940 at a major New York City art gallery (and even shown at an exhibit at

Gimbel's department store). From this point on her works were frequently exhibited throughout the U.S. and Europe in solo and group shows with favorable reviews. Her name "Grandma Moses" was also coined at this time, when the media found her life and work to be a great feature story. In a newspaper article that year she was quoted, "People tell me they're proud to be seen on the street with me. But I just say, well, why weren't you proud to be seen with me before? If people want to make a fuss over me, I just let 'em, but I was the same person before as I am now."

Her style, termed "American Primitive," was praised for its clarity of color, fidelity to detail, and simple but strong energy showing American rural life with telling accuracy. The underlying message of the basic virtues of family, church and community went over well with the public during the trying times of the Depression and the turbulent pre–World War II jitters. As far as her being a so-called "primitive," Grandma Moses wrote with her customary no-nonsense approach, "A primitive artist is an amateur whose work sells."

In various tributes, she was called the "grand old lady of American art" and an "authentic primitive."

Her paintings were also often reproduced on prints and licensed for greeting cards, textiles, and other items. Other painting titles included *The Old Oaken Bucket* and *From My Window.*

"What's the use of painting a picture if it isn't something nice," she wrote in her autobiography. "I think real hard till I think of something real pretty, and then I paint it. I like to paint old-timey things....there are a few left, and they are going fast. I do them all from memory, most of them are daydreams, as it were."

In 1949 President Harry Truman gave her the Women's National Press Club Award for outstanding accomplishment in art. Always modest, Grandma Moses commented on her success, "I am doing better work than at first, but it is owing to better brushes and paint." At a later tea with President Truman she even asked if he would play the piano—which he did.

Far from being a suffering and brooding artist, caught up in the angst of creation, she was steady and unimpressed by the fuss over her. She was also pleasantly surprised by the high prices accorded her creations.

Twice, Governor Nelson Rockefeller proclaimed "Grandma Moses Day" in New York in honor of her birthday. Accolades also came from President Truman and his successors as president through John F. Kennedy. She also corresponded with another painter—none other than Winston Churchill.

In another memorable quote of particular interest to seniors, she wrote:

> What a strange thing is memory, and hope; one looks backward, the other forward; one is of today, the other of tomorrow. Memory is history recorded in our brain, memory is a painter, it paints pictures of the past and of the day.

She passed away on Dec. 13, 1961 at the age of 101—but her work and role model live on.

Sir Henry Beecham
1879–1961

"There are two golden rules for an orchestra: start together and finish together. The public doesn't give a damn what goes on in between."

"Great music is that which penetrates the ear with facility and leaves the memory with difficulty. Magical music never leaves the memory."

These comments tend to exemplify the extraordinary musical career of Sir Henry Beecham, the famed English conductor.

Beecham kept conducting well past his 65th birthday. He conducted his last opera in Buenos Aires in 1958 when he was 79. The next year, at 80, he conducted at the Lucerne Festival. In early 1960, while in the U.S., he contracted pneumonia. But a few months later he was back conducting in London and expecting to complete an exacting summer schedule. His last conducting event was at Portsmouth, England that year. He died on March 8, 1961 at the age of 81, still planning future concerts.

During his latter years he also produced his biography, *A Mingled Chime,* in 1944, when he turned 65. Then in 1959 he wrote *Frederick Delius,* a biography of composer Frederick Delius, whose work he championed. He consistently sought to help other English composers along with Delius. Beecham was also married for the first time in 1944, with two other weddings to come.

Throughout his lengthy career he continued to give auditions to orchestra aspirants, both in England and in the many cities around the world where he performed. His travels, however, produced the quote (befitting his reputation for humor), "I have been all around the world and have formed a very poor opinion of it."

Overall there were 203 operatic productions in his career, as well as many recordings.

Beecham was born in St. Helens, England in 1879. He was well educated, including Oxford, but as far as music goes, he taught himself for the most part. Rather precociously, he studied Wagnerian opera scores at the tender age of seven, and put together an amateur orchestra of sorts when only 10. His first experience as a conductor came in 1910 in London. During World War I, he created the Beecham Opera Company.

Beecham's fame continued to grow, which helped him form the London Philharmonic Orchestra in 1932. Under his leadership this orchestra was soon considered one of the world's finer musical groups. In the same year he became artistic director of the Covent Garden Opera, also in London.

In 1936 Beecham took the London Philharmonic Orchestra on a tour of Germany. Adolf Hitler and other high German officials were in the audience in Berlin. Reportedly when Beecham saw Hitler applauding he commented to his orchestra, "The old bugger seems to like it." His quip apparently was transmitted over the radio throughout Europe, raising the issue of whether Beecham was fully aware the concert was being broadcast.

Beecham—a noted wit—was also reputed to have said after a personal session with Hitler, "Now I know what's wrong with Germany."

While initially poking fun at Hitler and Mussolini, in 1938 Beecham stopped any engagements in Germany. When World War II broke out he came to the U.S. and conducted in various cities, including the Metropolitan in New York. While he was criticized in Britain for leaving the country during the war, his reputation survived and then flourished again.

In 1946, back in London, he established the Royal Philharmonic Orchestra, which he managed for the rest of his life. In 1950 he took his new orchestra to the U.S. for a mammoth run of engagements: 52 concerts in 45 cities in 64 days.

In discussing his methods, Beecham said, "I just get the best players and let them play. At rehearsal they play the piece through; any mistakes they know about as well as I do, so we play it through again; then they know it. I know what they going to do…but they don't know what I'm going to do…so that at the performance everyone is on his toes, and we get a fine performance."

Among many honors, Beecham was knighted by the Queen of England for his services to English music. In 1938 the president of France awarded him the Legion of Honor. The Post Office of Great Britain, to mark the centennial of his birth, created a stamp with his likeness. A Sir Thomas Beecham Society was created by his American admirers to continue appreciation of his life and work.

Other noted quotes by Beecham include:

> *"A musicologist is a man who can read music but can't hear it."*

> *"Brass bands are all very well in their place—*
> *outdoors and several miles away."*

To a Liverpool concert audience:

> *"Ladies and gentlemen, in upwards of 50 years of concert-giving*
> *before the public, it has seldom been my good fortune*
> *to find the programme correctly printed.*
> *Tonight is no exception to the rule, and therefore,*
> *Ladies and Gentlemen, with your kind permission,*
> *we will now play the piece which you think*
> *you have just heard."*

> *"When the history of the first half of this century [the 20th century]*
> *is written—properly written—it will be acknowledged*
> *the most stupid and brutal in the history of civilization."*

Eleanor Roosevelt
1884–1962

"I would not be happy unless I had some regular work to do every day and I imagine that I will always feel that way no matter how old I am."

Eleanor Roosevelt was the wife of Franklin Delano Roosevelt, the 32nd president of the United States, whom she outlived by many years. FDR was elected to an unprecedented four terms as president, dying in office at the age of 63 in 1945. A distant cousin of FDR and the niece of Teddy Roosevelt, a former president, Eleanor Roosevelt assisted her husband through his many campaigns, his New Deal policies, which helped the nation recover from the Depression, and through the vicissitudes of World War II.

However, Eleanor Roosevelt achieved a remarkable record as a public servant in her own right, both as a diplomat and a humanitarian. Her many activities continued well past the 65 mark. From the outset of her public life she strived to improve housing for the poor, establish better health services, and pull up the status of minorities. Showing a flair for Americana, she was said to have shocked and surprised some people, including her mother-in-law, by serving hot dogs to the visiting king and queen of England.

She was one of the most respected and admired women in the world as well as the U.S., and a role model for generations of young women.

She and FDR had six children in 10 years. After FDR contracted polio in 1921 she became more active in the public arena. She began serving as an emissary for her husband and as a counselor and political helpmate while he was governor of New York. As First Lady during his four administrations as president (1933–1945), she elevated this position into one of great influence and magnitude. She was the initial First Lady to write a newspaper column ("My Day," begun in 1935 and continued for the rest of her life), make radio broadcasts, publish books and articles, and hold press conferences (for female reporters).

Extremely active, she even learned to fly with lessons from famed aviator Amelia Earhardt. But her plans to get a pilot's license ended with her husband's disapproval of that ambition.

During the war years she visited American armed forces on various fronts and also helped in civil defense work. Moreover, she was the first president's wife to travel the nation on speaking tours, chair national conferences in the White House, speak to national conventions, represent the country abroad, and even give a keynote address at her party's presidential convention. To some, critics and otherwise, she was deemed a presidential Cabinet member without portfolio.

One event that endeared her to many people was her decision in 1939 to resign from the Daughters of the American Revolution when the organization didn't permit Marian Anderson, an African-American singer, to perform in Constitution Hall. In 1945 she persuaded the Army Nurse Corps to take in black candidates. In the same year she joined the board of the National Association for the Advancement of Colored People (NAACP).

After FDR died, she called vice president Harry Truman and said, "Harry, the president is dead."

Truman, who succeeded Roosevelt as president, said, "Is there anything I can do for you?"

Eleanor Roosevelt, very much in character, responded: "Is there anything I can do for you? For you are the one in trouble now."

There was some talk of her running for senator from New York or for governor of the state. However, she was appointed a delegate to the newly formed United Nations, where she served 1945–1952 and again in 1961. She also became the chair of the United Nations Commission on Human Rights, 1946–1952, and assisted in the drafting of the "Universal Declaration of Human Rights" that she later helped get passed by the General Assembly. As a member of the United Nations Social, Humanitarian and Cultural Committee she argued successfully against the Soviet Union on the issue of refugee repatriation, calling for refugees in fear of political reprisal not to have to return to their country of origin.

In the postwar years, seeking to continue FDR's legacy as well as advance her positions, she lobbied for full employment legislation and national health insurance. She was firmly against segregation, championing its end in all forms. Moreover, she pushed for creation of a Civil Rights Division as part of the U.S. Department of Justice. She was also appointed to the advisory board of the Peace Corps.

In 1949, when 65, she went on TV with her daughter in *The Eleanor and Anna Show*, but the show failed to catch on and ended.

Outraged by the destructive antics of Senator Joseph McCarthy and the House Un-American Committee, she commented in 1950, "I want to be able to sit down with anyone who may have a new idea and not be afraid of contamination by association. In a democracy, you must be able to meet people and argue your point of view—people whom you have not screened beforehand. That must be part of the freedom of people in the United States."

Subsequently, in a further step to show her commitment to free expression, she became the honorary chairperson of Americans for Democratic Action.

At the age of 75 she took on a new assignment, flying from New York to Boston once a week to teach a course in international law and organization at Brandeis University. In early 1962, when 77, she flew to Europe and Israel to tape interviews for a television series called *Prospects of Mankind*. Her first guest on that show was Martin Luther King, Jr.

Her comment at 75 was apropos of her concept of public service: "When you cease to make a contribution, you begin to die."

Among the accolades she was given was being called the "First Lady of the Western World."

When President John F. Kennedy took office in 1960 she was soon appointed again as a delegate to the United Nations. She was also named chair of the President's Commission on the Status of Women. But her health began to fail, and she died in 1962.

Many honors have crowned and memorialized her life and work. She was buried next to her husband at their Hyde Park estate in upstate New York.

In a famous cartoon on the occasion of her 70th birthday, a little girl looks at the Statue of Liberty, and when questioned about its significance, tells her mother in the caption, "Of course I know—it's Mrs.

Roosevelt."

Her books include: *This Is My Story,* 1937; *My Days,* 1938; *This I Remember,* 1949 (when she turned 65); *On My Own,* 1958; *You Learn by Living,* 1960; and her *Autobiography* in 1961.

Of her Adlai Stevenson said, "She would rather light candles than curse the darkness."

Among her quotes/writings:

"One of the blessings of age is to learn not to part on a note of sharpness, to treasure the moments spent with those we love, and to make them whenever possible good to remember, for time is short."

"You gain strength, courage and confidence by every experience in which you really stop to look fear in the face. You must do the thing you think you cannot do."

"Only a man's character is the real opinion of worth."

"Character building begins in our infancy and continues until death."

"...perhaps it is as well to keep an open and charitable mind, and to try to understand why people do things instead of condemning the acts themselves."

"The giving of love is an education in itself."

"No one can make you feel inferior without your consent."

"What is to give light must endure the burning."

Robert Frost
1874–1963

"The woods are lovely, dark and deep,
But I have promises to keep,
And miles to go before I sleep,
And miles to go before I sleep."

These often-quoted and memorable lines come from Robert Frost's poem "Stopping by Woods on a Snowy Evening," which was one of the many famous poems written by Frost, generally considered to be the greatest American poet of the 20th century.

Over his long life Frost wrote many books of poetry and garnered a huge number of honors and awards, including four Pulitzer Prizes—becoming the first person to win four Pulitzers. He received so many honorary degrees that he eventually, through an admirer, had parts of the ceremonial garb woven into a quilt. A particularly distinctive honor came in the mid 1950s when the Vermont state legislature voted to name a mountain after him.

Frost's poems often reflected New England rural life and landscape in many ways, but with universal themes that made him much more than a regional poet. Using what he called "the sound of sense," he was able to craft poems that captured the cadence of New England speech while still writing in traditional verse forms. "We write of things we see and we write in accents we hear. Thus we gather both our material and our technique…"

Frost more than satisfied what he once described as his life's ambition, "To write a few poems it will be hard to get rid of." Some of his work addressed darker dimensions of the human condition, embodying the theme that creating form and harmony out of everyday life wards off the feeling of emptiness.

Many of his finest volumes came out after he was 65, though it became harder for him to focus as old age advanced and he faced medical difficulties including cancer of the prostrate. This trove includes

A Winter Tree, published in 1942 when he was 66, and for which he received his fourth and last Pulitzer in 1943. *Come In & Other Poems* came out in 1943. *A Masque of Reason* was published in 1945; *Steeple Bush* in 1947, and *Aforesaid* in 1954. *In the Clearing,* his ninth and last collection of poems, was published in 1962, when he was 88.

In 1958 he was appointed Consultant in Poetry to the Library of Congress, with Congress later also awarding him a Gold Medal. In 1961 he recited a special poem, "The Gift Outright," at the inauguration of President John F. Kennedy.

Over his career Frost gave many readings of his work. In his latter years he began to recite his poems from memory rather than read them due to poor eyesight. In 1953 he had surgery for a recurrence of skin cancer on his face.

Frost was born in San Francisco in 1874. His family moved to a farm in New England when he was 10. He had stints as a reporter for a local newspaper and teaching at several schools. He also married. He and his wife, Elinor, had six children, with two dying in infancy.

The first poem for which he was paid was published in 1894. When the farm didn't do well, he decided to allocate more time and energy to his writings in England. In 1912 they rented a cottage near London, and the very next year an English publisher came out with *A Boy's Will.*

With the onslaught of World War I the family returned to the U.S., where they bought a farm at Franconia, New Hampshire. His stature as a poet was well established by this time, and he began giving talks and readings. In the 1920s he was considered one of the major, if not the most prominent, poet in the U.S. He also began two long-term relationships. One was teaching at Amherst University, which he did off and on for many years; the other was with the publisher Henry Holt & Company, which published all of his subsequent books for the rest of his life. There is a Robert Frost Library at Amherst University.

During the 1930s he faced several family crises—his wife and a daughter died, and a son committed suicide—but he kept writing.

At the behest of the State Department he became a good will ambassador, going on missions to Brazil in 1954, Britain in 1957, and Greece in 1961. He also had a famous session with Premier Khrushchev in Moscow, during which he made some impromptu political comments (which he added to right after landing back in the U.S.); his statements were criticized and soured his relationship with President Kennedy.

Frost died on Jan. 29, 1963 at the age of 89. He was buried in a family plot in Old Bennington, Vermont.

Among his quotes:

"Love is an irresistible desire to be irresistibly desired."

"A mother takes 20 years to make a man of her boy, and another woman makes a fool of him in 20 minutes."

"Education is the ability to listen to almost anything without losing your temper."

"I never dared to be radical when young for fear it would make me conservative when old."

"In three words I can sum up everything I've learned about life. It goes on."

General Douglas MacArthur
1880–1964

*"**Age** wrinkles the body. **Quitting** wrinkles the soul."*

Born into a military family in Little Rock, Arkansas, with a father who was a general in the army and a demanding mother who expected greatness of him, Douglas MacArthur became a legend in his own time— but a highly controversial one. Invariably sure of himself, MacArthur sought and gained praise, but some derision came, too, as reflected in this part of a soldier's ditty, which ended:

> *And while possibly a rumor now,*
> *Some day it will be a fact*
> *That the Lord will hear a deep voice say,*
> *"Move over, God, it's Mac."*

MacArthur served the U.S. both domestically and abroad for 52 years, primarily in the Far East. He was generally considered to be a brilliant military strategist. As a military statesman and politician, however, his standing is more mixed. He was often criticized for being headstrong and disobeying orders, which finally proved his undoing.

He graduated from West Point, where he later served as superintendent, in 1903 as first in his class. His first post was in the Philippines, where he spent a good deal of time during his career. He fought in World War I, received various medals for bravery, and advanced quickly in the military hierarchy. Charged in 1932 with restoring order at Washington D.C. when a "Bonus Army" of disgruntled World War I veterans sought early payment of a promised bonus, he was accused of overly aggressive measures (burning shelters and the use of gas).

Between marriages he had a Eurasian mistress when he was 54 and a four-star general. His second marriage led to a son, a source of

136

much pride in his later years.

MacArthur returned to the Philippines prior to World War II. But as commander of military forces in the Philippines he was criticized for not preparing effectively for the imminent Japanese invasion of the islands. Some soldiers nicknamed him "Dugout Doug" for staying in greater safety in Corregidor rather than in Bataan, but his survival was considered paramount, and he was finally evacuated to Australia after issuing his famed promise of "I shall return."

MacArthur was already 65 when World War II ended in 1945 (he actually reentered Manila shortly after his 65th birthday). After helping pave the way for Philippine independence, he was named Supreme Occupation Commander of defeated Japan in August 1945. He was quoted as saying this command was "Mars' last gift to an old war dog." Despite criticism of his autocratic ways, and that he didn't create the reforms that helped demilitarize Japan and turn it into a democracy, it was on his watch that his seven-point plan for post-war Japan bore fruit. Among his acts were giving the vote to Japanese women and prompting the creation of labor unions. The Japanese, for the most part, admired MacArthur, and credited him with helping the nation recover from the war and achieve stability and progress.

MacArthur spent six years in Tokyo, always sensitive to criticism while often ignoring it. "My major advisors now have boiled down to almost two men—George Washington and Abraham Lincoln. One founded the United States, the other saved it. If you go back in their lives, you can find almost all the answers."

He was also fond of a saying, found at his desk, "Youth is not a time of life—it's a state of mind." His work in his old age, despite the impact on his body and mind of long hours and mental strain (though he usually concluded he was right after his analysis of any problem), reflected his belief in this adage.

MacArthur had political ambitions that stretched to the White House. Some influential members of the Republican Party were interested in getting him the 1948 nomination to run for president. However, MacArthur basically preferred to remain in Tokyo and maintain his "mystique" rather than risk being another "political target" if he came back to the U.S. to actually campaign himself for the nomination. To run for office would also mean resigning from the Army, something he didn't want to do. Subsequently, he fared poorly in a Wisconsin primary he had been favored to win, and his drive to the Republican nomination stalled. Interestingly, many Japanese supported his presidential ambitions.

While he might have retired around this time, the North Koreans invaded South Korea in June 1950. At the age of 70 he still received command of the United Nations' military force when it was determined to reverse the North Korean invasion. However, MacArthur quickly differed from administration policy on broad strategic terms. MacArthur wanted to use Nationalist Chinese troops from Formosa/Taiwan (where they had retreated after losing the mainland war to the Red Chinese arny), bomb Manchuria, and if necessary use the atomic bomb against the People's Republic of China. The administration was leery of provoking the Chinese, or the Soviet Union, into the conflict and possibly creating a much wider war; MacArthur, however, argued that the U.S. shouldn't fight a limited war.

MacArthur was overly optimistic over defeating the North Korean forces, as he had been accused of being during World War II campaigns against the Japanese. One quote attributed to him indicated that "all he had to do was send a few Americans over there and the North Koreans would run." But events on the battlefield proved him wrong, and the U.N. troops were initally forced to retreat. But finally the U.N. soldiers were able to stabilize the situation and avoid being evacuated. Despite opposition by other military leaders about the viability of his daring plan to stage an amphibious landing at Inchon behind enemy lines (high tides and mud flats being among other obstacles), MacArthur received approval and the landing was both the surprise he sought and a huge success.

Again over-optimistic as the U.N. forces beat the North Koreans back over the 38th parallel, which divided the two parts of the Korean peninsula, MacArthur sought permission to pursue the enemy to the Yalu River, the border with Manchuria/Red China. To establish clarity of mutual purpose President Truman and MacArthur met on Wake Island in October 1951. MacArthur thought the war would soon end, and he predicted the Chinese wouldn't dare enter the fray, though it soon became clear he had badly underestimated Chinese intentions and resources. He also sought to allay any Truman suspicions on his political aspirations. One relevant quote, "If you have a general running against you, his name will be Eisenhower, not MacArthur."

Overriding commands to desist sending American troops to the Yalu River and only use South Korean forces, MacArthur dispatched U.S. units that far north and also risked dividing the Allied troops. The Chinese did enter the war, with large numbers, inflicting many casualties on the U.N. forces, who were driven south beneath the 38th parallel. While the administration wanted to find a way to end the conflict with a compromise that preserved the independence of South Korea, MacArthur desired to bring the war to a successful conclusion, even if it meant extending the conflict beyond South Korea, as he saw it as a major means to end the world-wide threat of communism. His public comments, at odds with administration policy (including an ultimatum to China), finally brought Truman to a controversial decision to relieve him of his command and issue his recall. MacArthur was hardly surprised and planned to come back to the U.S.—where he hadn't been for 14 years—to defend himself and perhaps still win the presidency. He was met by adoring crowds in San Francisco and New York, where he moved into a luxurious Waldorf Astoria suite, which was provided at nominal rent ($450 a month) and which became his home for the rest of his life. As a five-star general, he retained his 1951 salary (over $18,000) as well as his rank and active status.

In his famous farewell address to Congress, MacArthur summarized his positions in a 34-minute speech that included such memorable lines as: Once a conflict begins, "there can be no substitute for victory;" and, referring to an old barracks ballad, "Old soldiers never die; they just fade away. And like the soldier of that ballad, I now close my military career and just fade away—an old soldier who tried to do his duty as God gave him the light to see that duty. Goodbye."

However, far from fading away, MacArthur remained active. He delivered the keynote address at the 1952 Republican convention, hoping that a deadlock might arise that could still yield him the nomination. But Eisenhower was nominated on the first ballot. Inconclusive hearings were held by the Senate on his recall, where he testified without admitting any errors on his part. Despite his advanced age he went on a national speaking tour while sending out press releases outlining his positions on foreign policy issues.

On Aug. 1, 1952 he accepted a position as board chairman of the Remington Rand Corporation (later Sperry Rand and then Unisys) and ceased being a player in the political scene. As an elder statesman he was still consulted by two more presidents. He warned President John F. Kennedy regarding growing involvement in the Vietnam morass and sending U.S. troops to fight on the Asian mainland. One quote on the issue: "All the chickens are coming home to roost and you are living in the coop." Reportedly he repeated the same point about Vietnam to President Lyndon Johnson as well.

When past 75 he pointed out how the nature of war had changed since he entered the Army at the turn of the century, and that it had become a means of total annihilation, possibly of all sides. War, he declared, was no longer a practical means of settling "international differences." Accordingly, abolishing war had become an issue that all sides should agree upon, as they would all benefit equally.

After being out of the public eye for a decade. MacArthur's death in March 1964 brought another large outpouring of public tribute. His book *Reminisces* was published in 1964, when he was 84. Later that year he died. American flags were lowered to half-mast for six days as the nation went into mourning.

"In war there is no substitute for victory."

"A general is just as good or just as bad as the troops under his command."

"There is no security on this earth; there is only opportunity."

"No man is entitled to the blessings of freedom unless he be vigilant in its preservation."

Winston Churchill
1874–1965

"It has been said that democracy
is the worst form of government
except for all the others that have been tried."

Winston Churchill was one of the greatest figures of the 20th century. He was a man of prodigious talents, both as a statesman who led England to victory in World War II, and as a writer who was awarded the Nobel Prize for Literature in 1953 when he was 79.

Churchill was born in Blenheim Palace in Woodstock on Nov. 30, 1874 to an English father and American mother (Jennie Jerome). After schooling he went into the British Army and fought in northwest India and the Sudan. Subsequently he left the army and became a war correspondent, covering the Boer War in South Africa. He wrote tellingly of his war experiences.

He served 64 years as a member of the House of Commons in the English Parliament, starting in 1900. He also held several important Cabinet positions, though he generated some adverse opinions on his loyalty as he switched political parties. As First Lord of the Admiralty he led naval expansion before World War I, but then lost his post after the disastrous Dardanelles campaign in Turkey during the war, which failed badly with great losses.

While his party was out of power between the world wars (the period of 1929–1939 was dubbed his "wilderness years"), he tried to convince England to take a stronger position against Hitler, the Nazis, and a rearming Germany. When the second world conflict finally ensued he was named First Lord of the Admiralty again, with a signal sent to the fleet that "Winston is back." Soon afterwards, in his mid-sixties, he became prime minister and an inspirational wartime leader of the country.

During his declining years he was said to have been plagued by fits of depression, which he termed his "black dogs." But with his indomitable spirit, he kept writing and painting. Even in his old age he was able to recite long passages of favorite poems he had committed to memory as a young man.

He suffered a stroke on Jan. 15, 1965 and died nine days later. His body lay in state at Westminster Hall for three days, and he was honored by the first British state funeral for a commoner since 1914. He was buried, at his request, at Saint Martin's Churchyard, Bladon, near Woodstock in Oxfordshire.

Proficient in both written and spoken English, Churchill coined many famed statements, some humorous and some with more gravitas. He told one woman who accused him of being inebriated, "And you, madam, are ugly. But in the morning I shall be sober."

Referring to his passion for history, he stated, "History will not be kind to me, for I intend to write it."

As far as his safety—assassination attempts were a threat—he quipped, "Although prepared for martyrdom, I prefer that it be postponed."

Even as a young man he had recognized the power of oratory, and wrote, "Of all the talents bestowed upon men, none is so precious as the gift of oratory. He who enjoys it wields a power more durable than that of a great king."

On the advent of his 75th birthday, he declared, "I am ready to meet my Maker; whether my Maker is prepared for the ordeal of meeting me is another matter."

Perhaps his most uplifting statement was,

Every day you may make progress. Every step may be fruitful. Yet there will stretch out before you an ever lengthening, ever-ascending, ever-improving path. You know you will never get to the end of the journey. But this, so far from discouraging, only adds to the joy and glory of the climb.

A Churchill Museum, the major center dedicated to his life, is housed in the Cabinet War Headquarters, his World War II underground center.

Among his many other quotes:

"A fanatic is one who cannot change his mind
and won't change the subject."

"A lie gets half way around the world before the truth
has a chance to get its pants on."

"An appeaser is one who feeds a crocodile, hoping it will eat him last."

"From now on, ending a sentence with a preposition
is something up with which I won't put."

"Men occasionally stumble over the truth,
but most of them pick themselves up and hurry off
as if nothing ever happened."

"I like pigs.
Dogs look up to us.
Cats look down on us.
Pigs treat us as equals."

W. Somerset Maugham
1874–1965

*"Most people cannot see anything, but I can see
what is in front of my nose with extreme clearness;
the greatest writers can see through a brick wall.
My vision is not so penetrating."*

Despite this modest statement as to his literary prowess, W. Somerset Maugham was one of the greatest writers of the 20th century, continuing to churn out fiction well past his 65th birthday and until his death at the age of 91.

His work continued despite some health problems. At 84 he required a surgical glove to write due to a severe writer's cramp condition. Unhappy over his hearing aid, he was said to have tossed it into the Mediterranean in a fit of pique. He also endured a hernia operation, and was one of the major figures who undertook cellular therapy treatments at Vevey, Switzerland—which involved transplantation of cells from sheep fetuses to replace or revitalize waning organs. (Charles Chaplin was another luminary to sample this treatment.)

Maugham was considered the highest paid writer in the world in the 1930s. Quite a few of his novels and short stories (78 books in total) were made into movies, including *Rain, The Moon and Sixpence* and *The Razor's Edge.*

The Summing Up, his autobiography, came out in 1938. *The Razor's Edge,* a novel, was published in 1944 when he was 70. *Quartet,* four short stories, appeared in 1948. A special republication of his early novel *Cakes and Ale* came out on a celebration of his 80th birthday. At 80 he also had *Ten Novels & Their Authors* published, which consisted of articles on his choices for the 10 greatest novels ever written.

Then and Now, a historical novel, came out in 1947 when he was over 70. *Creatures of Circumstance,* his last collection of stories, was published in 1947. His last novel, *Catalina,* was published in 1948.

144

He published his last book in 1959 at the age of 85—*Points of View,* a collection of essays.

Maugham was born in Paris (his first language was French) but at age 10 moved to London as an orphan to live with an uncle. He was trained as a doctor, and his experiences in the London slums, which undoubtedly sharpened his powers of observation, led to his first novel, *Liza of Lambeth.* Success of the novel led to his decision to pursue a literary rather than a medical career.

Maugham also wrote many plays. In 1908 he had four plays running at the same time in London. One of his best known novels, *Of Human Bondage,* which was semi-autobiographical, came out in 1915. At the outbreak of World War I he was 40 and a bit old for a soldier, but he had a stint as a British Red Cross ambulance driver in France. Later during the conflict he performed some work for British Intelligence in Geneva, and then in Petrograd during the Russian revolution in 1917. His novel *Ashendon, or the British Agent* was based to some extent on his experiences as an intelligence agent, and may have been a precursor to the spy story genre.

Maugham traveled extensively, especially to the South Pacific, and over his career became easily the most widely traveled writer of his time. *The Moon and Sixpence,* based on the life of painter Paul Gauguin, came out in 1919. He also wrote travel books, including *On a Chinese Screen* and *The Gentleman in the Parlor.*

At the outset of World War II Maugham wrote some material at the request of the British government, with the articles collected in a 1940 book, *France at War.* He also made speeches for the BBC. Subsequently he lived in the U.S. during the conflict, first in South Carolina and later in Hollywood. He also wrote articles and made speeches to help the war effort. In addition, he donated the original manuscript of his novel *Of Human Bondage* to the Library of Congress.

After the war he returned to Europe at the age of 72, and as a token of his advanced age he began referring to himself as a "Very Old Party." He returned to his luxurious (tennis court and pool, among other creature comforts) 12-acre villa on Cap Ferrat on the French Riviera, where he had established his permanent home (called Villa Mauresque) in the 1930s. Again he held court with many notables in various fields. He died in Nice in December 1965, after reputedly seeking reassurance that there was no life after death.

Some believed he should have been a candidate for a Nobel Prize in literature. Always a realist, Maugham wrote of himself,

> I have never pretended to be anything but a story teller. It has amused me to tell stories and I have told a great many. It is a misfortune for me that the telling of a story just for the sake of a story is not an activity that is in favor with the intelligentsia.

Throughout his life Maugham was said to have struggled with his sexual nature, with relationships with both women and men, though his nature tilted to men during the latter part of his life.

Struck by the foibles of mankind, Maugham once wrote, "The ordinary is the writer's richest field."

Other salient quotes:

"What makes old age hard to bear is not the failing of one's faculties, but the burden of one's memories."

"Impropriety is the soul of wit."

"Money is like a sixth sense without which one cannot make a complete use of the other five."

"There are three rules for writing the novel. Unfortunately, no one knows what they are."

"Love is the only dirty trick played on us to achieve continuation of the species."

"An unfortunate thing about this world is that the good habits are much easier to give up than the bad ones."

"Excess on occasion is exhilarating. It prevents moderation from acquiring the deadening effect of a habit."

"Tradition is a guide and not a jailor."

"It wasn't until late in life that I discovered how easy it was to say 'I don't know.'"

"If you refuse to accept anything but the best, very often you get it."

JACK ADLER

"Imagination grows by exercise, and contrary to common belief,
is more powerful in the mature than in the young."

"Dying is a very dull, dreary affair.
And my advice to you is to have nothing whatever to do with it."

Le Corbusier
1887–1965

"A curved street is a donkey track; a straight street, a road for men."

Le Corbusier, one of the most outstanding architects and city planners of the 20th century, continued to work on new projects until the end of his long life.

His real name was Charles-Eduard Jeanneret-Gris. He was born in 1887 in the Swiss watch-making town of La Chaux-de-Fonds. After some training as an artist, and travel throughout Europe to learn more about architectural styles, he settled in Paris in 1917. Subsequently he began to develop his own architectural theories, with some on the avant-garde side. He believed that growing industrialization called for a new style of architecture, and the end of World War I provided an opportunity. "We must start from zero," he said.

Accordingly, he was a pioneer in more functional architecture, using reinforced concrete, which centered on the concept of the house as a "machine for living." In explanation of his theory, criticized for its technocratic applications, he said much later,

> A thousand utterances have been produced to beat me for having dared that utterance. But when I say "living" I am not talking of mere material requirements only. I admit certain important extensions which must crown the edifice of man's daily needs. To be able to think, or meditate, after the day's work is essential. But in order to become a centre of creative thought, the home must take on an absolutely new character.

He also developed a style utilizing a concrete skeleton-like structure for multi-story buildings. His "Dom-ino" theory (combining "domicile" and "innovation") centered around structures where components could possibly be assembled as pieces that could be moved as in a game of dominoes.

At one point he proposed a radical change to one part of Paris by replacing what was there with a large number of 60-story towers.

Along with others he wrote various articles about architecture that were incorporated in a 1917 book, *Towards a New Architecture.* He and the other authors used pseudonyms. He chose "Le Corbusier," the name of a paternal ancestor, a nom de plume he used for the rest of his life.

In 1922 he put forward his principle of the "radiating city," which featured large housing units separated by gardens from auto and pedestrian traffic. He visualized new cities, managed by experts, as elements of greater societal order without urban sprawl. Decorative objects and ornamentation considered wasteful would be replaced by more utilitarian objects. His city planning, however, was considered by some to be a form of anti-social urbanism, and criticized for destroying city life by eliminating areas of public contact and participation like cafes and churches to concentrate on more self-contained living units.

In 1930 he participated in a competition for a "Green City" outside Moscow intended as a rest and recuperation area for workers. But his plans hardly fit the tenor of the Soviet state by calling for independent apartments set off from collective pressures.

Many of his most famous works came after World War II. He often sought to reconcile the elements of modernization with local building styles while providing living quarters amid organized traffic- and garden-like areas and arteries.

Among structures he designed when past 65 were Notre-Dame-du-Haut at Ronchamp, France, the Philips Pavilion in Brussels, the National Museum of Western Art in Tokyo, the Congress Palace in Strasbourg, the French Embassy in Brasilia and the Carpenter Center for the Visual Arts at Harvard University.

A skillful sculptor and painter, Le Corbusier also wrote books on interior decoration and painting as well as architecture. His books include *The City of Tomorrow* in 1929 and *The Three Human Establishments,* 1945. In 1954, when he was 67, *The Modular* came out.

On his first visit to Manhattan, in 1935, he thought the city's skyscrapers were too small. His less-than-glittering impressions of the

U.S. appeared in a 1937 allegory, *When the Cathedrals Were White: A Journey to the Country of Timid People.* The superiority and leadership of France in such cultural matters throughout the world was a constant element of his writings and commentaries.

Two lesser known books, written during the Vichy period of World War II (1940–1942), were *The Four Routes and The Home of Man.*

He was also an architectural advisor, including a project near the end of his career for the construction of a state capital of Chandigarh for the Indian state of Punjab. This was the first time he was able to apply his principles of city planning.

Le Corbusier was still very much active when he died in a swimming accident at Cap Martin on the French Riviera in 1965 when he was 78. He was given a state funeral. In 1968, a Corbusier Foundation was established to commemorate his life and works. But his memory is best exemplified by the structures he created.

Among his famed sayings were:

"A hundred times have I thought New York is a catastrophe, and 50 times that it is a beautiful catastrophe."

"I prefer drawing to talking. Drawing is faster, and leaves less room for lies."

"Architecture is the learned game, correct and magnificent, of forms assembled in the light."

"The home should be the treasure chest of living."

"Space and light and order. These are the things that men need as much as they need bread or a place to sleep."

"Genius is personal, decided by fate; but it expresses itself by means of system. There is no work of art without system."

Jean Arp
1887–1966

"Art is a fruit that grows in man,
like a fruit on a plant,
like a child in its mother's womb."

Jean Arp, a French-German sculptor, painter and poet, was one of the most dominant and influential artists of the 20th century. His work—embracing different art movements including Dadaism, Surrealism and Abstraction-Creationism—came in many forms, including sculptures, bas-reliefs and collages. Many museums around the world exhibit his creations, some possessing a humorous touch. His work has also been used in many posters. Over six decades of creative activity comprised several volumes of poetry, in both French and German. Composers also created some musical compositions based on his poems.

Arp continued working well beyond the 65 mark. In 1950, when he was nearly 65, he created a monument relief in wood and metal at the Harvard Graduate Center in Cambridge, Massachusetts. Four years later, in 1954, he was awarded the grand prize for sculpture at the Venice Biennale. Other honors also came in his later years, including the Grand Prix National des Arts in 1963 and the Carnegie Prize in 1964. He was made a chevalier of the French Legion of Honor in 1960. In 1958, when he was 71, he created a mural relief for the UNESCO Building in Paris.

As a poet and essayist he continued writing his entire life, with much of his work appearing in magazines. Never resting on his laurels, or losing a certain humorous approach, Arp continued being innovative while working on new forms of sculpture, collages, ink designs on paper, et al. His last self-portrait was finished in 1965.

Arp was born in Strasbourg in the Alsace-Lorraine region in 1887. His mother was French-Alsatian and his father, German. At this time, after the Franco-Prussian war, the territory had been taken over by Germany; hence, his name was Hans. But the region was returned to France at the end of World War I, and the French government directed that his name become Jean, which is the first name generally used with him. Many people, getting around the name issue, just called him "Arp."

He, himself, tended to speak French with his mother and German with his father, and in the Alsatian dialect when the family was together. In later years he sometimes translated poems originally written in German into French.

Arp's first sculpture, in wood, came at the precocious age of eight. Subsequently, he studied in both Strasbourg and Paris. He became one of the founders of the Dada movement in Europe before World War I. In the Dada credo, many artists rebelled against traditional art and literature forms and created purposefully irrational and non-recognizable works. In his early collages, shown in a 1915 exhibit, Arp used such new materials as wool, silk, cloth and paper.

He lived in Paris, Cologne and Zurich and finally settled in Meudon, a Paris suburb, in 1926. Several years earlier, in 1922, he married Sophie, a fellow artist. They sometimes worked together in creating art pieces.

The Dada school evolved into Surrealism in the 1920s. In this movement, artists used their subconscious to create works that had no logical or easily understandable form. But in 1931 Arp departed from surrealism to found the Abstraction-Creationism movement, which led to his works having a more geometrical form. Arp felt that his sculpture was still "concrete rather than abstract," as it did occupy space.

In 1941 he had a collection of poems, *Poems Without Pronouns,* published.

In 1942, after the onset of World War II, Arp fled France to live in Zurich and neutral Switzerland. After the war he returned to Meudon in 1946. His first visit to the U.S. came in 1949. He died in 1966 in Solduno, Switzerland. But his works live on in museums, art and book collections and in posters that are collectors' items.

There is an Arp Museum in Rolandseck, Germany and a Jean Arp Foundation in Clamart, France. His writings can be read in *Arp on Arp: Poems, Essays, Memories (Documents of 20th Century Art)* and *Hans Arp.*

One of Arp's comments on the artistic process:

"Anyone who tries to shoot down a cloud with arrows will soon exhaust
his quiver. Many sculptors are like these foolish hunters.
Here is what one should do: charm the cloud
with the tune of a violin played on a drum,
or with the tune of a drum played on a violin.
Then before long the cloud will come down
and take its ease on earth until,
full of happiness, it turns to stone.
Thus in the twinkling of an eye
the sculptor realizes his
most beautiful works."

Charles de Gaulle
1890–1970

"How can anyone govern a nation
that has 246 different cheeses?"

Charles de Gaulle was a seminal figure in France and the world scene as the leader of the Free French Forces during World War II and then later as president of France. Towering in size—he was six foot, five inches tall—as well as authority, he helped stabilize France and, to some extent, restore the nation as a major player in world diplomacy. Much of his part in French politics came after he was 65, and he overcame cataract operations in 1952 and 1956. He also survived an assassination attempt in 1962 by disgruntled members of the OAS *(Organization Armee Secrete)* who wanted to keep Algeria as part of France.

De Gaulle was born in Lille in 1890. He graduated from the French military academy of St. Cyr in 1912, where one nickname for him was "the tall asparagus." During World War I he was wounded several times. Captured by the Germans at the great battle of Verdun, he made five unsuccessful attempts at escape (his height tended to give him away). He was a prisoner of war for 32 months, including solitary confinement as punishment for his tries at escape. He used his imprisonment to enhance his education, study German, write a book, and give lectures to keep his fellow prisoners alert and active.

After the war he lectured on military history at the war college and lobbied for a mobile defense strategy based on the tank. His position was opposed by other military leaders who favored static fortifications, most notably the Maginot Line, on the border with Germany. Some fellow officers referred to him as the "motorized colonel." De Gaulle's theories proved correct when the German panzers succeeded in going around the French fortifications at the beginning of World War II.

Skilled as a writer as well as a military tactician, de Gaulle wrote several books between the two world wars. *Discord Among the Enemy*, about the relationship between civil and military powers in Germany, came out in 1924. *The Edge of the Sword*, covering his lectures on leadership, appeared in 1932. *The Army of the Future* came out in 1934, and *France and Her Army* in 1938.

In 1921 he married his wife, Yvonne; they had three children.

After the fall of France in 1940, De Gaulle refused to capitulate. While the Germans occupied Paris De Gaulle fled to London and made his famed "summons" to the French people to continue the struggle. By this time he had become a brigadier general and had served as an undersecretary of war. In effect, he constituted himself the leader of the Free French Resistance. This led to the Vichy government in France, which favored an armistice with the thus far victorious Germans, to sentence him *in absentia* to death for treason.

While he had his differences with Churchill, and especially Roosevelt (who considered him a prima donna), his role grew in importance during the course of the war. De Gaulle maintained that while he often disagreed with Churchill, they understood each other; whereas he seldom argued with Roosevelt, but the two leaders never understood each other.

With the liberation of France he was selected to head the provisional government that was set up. However, disgusted with the political maneuverings that went on and the weakness of presidential powers, he resigned in 1946 and went to his home at Colombey-des-Deux-Eglises to work on his memoirs.

The 1958 coup d'etat in Algeria, which was considered an integral part of France (by the French, not the Algerians), brought de Gaulle out of retirement when he was 68. Many in France were afraid of a civil war between supporters of retaining Algeria and those prepared to grant the Algerians independence. De Gaulle was elected president of the Fifth French Republic, with a strong mandate including a reformed constitution and special powers. The new constitution, which among other elements allowed him to rule by decree in emergencies, was approved by 83 per cent of the electorate.

Subsequently, his administration strengthened the French economy and created considerable prosperity. On the international front, he managed to get a referendum passed granting independence to Algeria, survived an attempted but short-lived coup by some generals, and then had his car shot at near Paris in a failed assassination by those who wanted Algeria kept as part of France. He then transformed France's other African colonies into independent states to prevent any more drives for national status.

Always mindful of achieving a major role for France in international affairs, de Gaulle had France leave NATO while developing a French nuclear strike capability, with the country's first atomic bomb exploded in 1960. Increasingly, de Gaulle opposed American and British policies, seeking to create a stronger and more independent Europe and to also avoid a two-power world of the U.S. and the Soviet Union.

In 1962 he threatened to resign if an amendment to the constitution allowing popular vote/universal suffrage instead of elections through an electoral college failed. The amendment passed by a large margin.

At age 75 De Gaulle was reelected in 1965, with greater presidential powers as a result of the referendum. But his prestige plummeted to a degree with domestic problems. High prices and unemployment led to labor strikes and student uprisings ("Make Love, Not War" was one of the famous slogans) which plagued his administration, and led to calls for his resignation. Even with the turmoil de Gaulle, ever imbued with Gallic pride, felt some admiration in the power of the students to trigger social unrest. "Naturally, it had to happen here. Paris is still the intellectual capital of the world."

Comments about the Jews "being an elite people, self-confident, and domineering" in a 1967 speech after the Six-Day War between Israel and Arab states led to him being accused, in some quarters, of fomenting anti-Semitism while trying to curry favor with Arab leaders. A call for independence for French-speaking Quebec in 1967 was also quite controversial.

In 1969 he resigned over the failure of a referendum on more constitutional reform, and he resumed his retirement. He worked on his memoirs and watched rugby matches on television, despairing when France lost. He died of natural causes in 1970, just shy of his 80th birthday.

De Gaulle's strengthening of France lives on, as do his three volume memoirs: *The Call to Honor* covering 1940–1942; *Unity*, 1942–44; and *Salvation*, 1944–46. De Gaulle Airport in Paris is one of the many places bearing his name.

Among his many quotes:

"I have come to the conclusion that politics are too serious a matter to be left to the politicians."

"In order to become the master, the politician poses as the servant."

"Patriotism is when love of your own people comes first; nationalism when hate for people other than your own comes first."

"Deliberation is the work of many men. Action, of one alone."

"A man of character finds a special attractiveness in difficulty, since it is only by coming to grips with difficulty that he can realize his potentialities."

"I respect those who resist me, but I cannot tolerate them."

"Nothing can be done without great men. And you become a great man only by wanting to be one."

Reinhold Niebuhr
1892–1971

"Man's capacity for justice makes democracy possible, but man's inclination to injustice makes democracy necessary."

Reinhold Niebuhr was a writer, philosopher, and Protestant theologian whose writings centered on relating the tenets of Christianity to the truths of human nature and the realities of modern politics, diplomacy, and world events. He continued in this task of establishing the relevance of Christianity to contemporary issues, and trying to develop a moral basis for social/political action, well past his 65th birthday in 1957, despite increasingly poor health.

In his teachings, Niebuhr argued that people were better able to be ethical when they understood how simple it was for their motives to become bad, and that the right path in human behavior came with the understanding that God, and not man, was sovereign. Society and social groupings, he averred, could create the potential to lead people into evil. However, Christianity possessed the values that could provide reform of people and society, though it shouldn't be considered a crutch against misfortune and problems. Under "Christian realism," people should avoid being too utopian or too resigned over human destiny. He was critical of Americans for losing touch with early virtues and values.

"To understand himself truly means to begin with a faith that he is understood from beyond himself, that he is known and loved of God and must find himself in terms of obedience to the divine will," Niebuhr wrote. Humanity had to understand the dangers of pride and the impact of society.

Man, being more than a natural creature, is not interested merely in physical survival but in prestige and social approval. Having the intelligence to anticipate the perils in which he stands in nature and history, he invariably seeks to gain security against these perils by enhancing his power, individually and collectively.

The paradox that can emerge is that "security through power means insecurity for those who lack power."

In 1958, when he was 66, he came out with the book *Press & Secular America*. The next year saw his book *Structure of Nations & Empires*. In 1963, a co-authored *A Nation So Conceived: Reflections on the History of America from the Early Visions to the Present Power*. Another volume, *Man's Nature & His Communities: Essays on the Dynamics & Enigmas of Man's Personal & Social Existence*, came out in 1965. His last book, *The Democratic Experience: Past & Prospects*, was issued in 1969.

Though seriously ill in his latter years, even at one point requiring psychiatric help for depression, he remained busy. Activities included being a consultant to the Fund for the Republic and the Ford Foundation, work for Columbia University's Institute of War & Peace Studies, and the Center for Foreign Policy Research in Washington D.C. A 1960–61 Rockefeller Foundation grant enabled him to begin another book. He also taught at Union Theological Seminary in New York until 1960, when he was 68. In 1961 he conducted lectures at Harvard.

Niebuhr was not a fan of President Richard Nixon or the Vietnam War, and he was always a foe of undue complacency in religious practices. From his sickbed he satirized Nixon's innovation in 1969 of Sunday worship services at the White House presided over by various religious figures in "the King's Chapel & the King's Court." He also quipped about the impact of "what a simple White House invitation will do to dull the critical faculties."

He was considered by many to be one of America's greatest political philosophers. Vice President Hubert Humphrey paid him a great tribute, saying, "No preacher or teacher, at least in my time, has had a greater impact on the secular world. No American has made a greater contribution to political wisdom and moral responsibility."

Niebuhr was born in Wright City, Missouri in 1882. He was the son of a German-American pastor, and he decided to also join the ministry. In 1915 he was ordained a pastor in the Evangelical Church. He served as a pastor in Detroit for 13 years; the experience had a tremendous impact on him. Unregulated factory and assembly line work conditions led him into an appreciation of socialism. He became a founder of the Fellowship of Socialist Christians. He also married, and subsequently had a son and daughter.

In 1928 he became a Professor of Practical Theology at the Union Theological Seminary in New York City, where he taught until retirement in 1960. The next year he described his Detroit experiences in *Leaves from the Notebook of a Tamed Cynic*. Several years later his first major work, *Moral Man & Immoral Society*, was published.

He drew away from standard socialist and liberal viewpoints in favor of an ideology he termed "Christian Realism," which sought to apply the beliefs of Christianity into social, economic and political areas. Religion, he argued, should function as a moral referee of sorts between the demands of labor and capital. As a journalist, he founded a magazine in 1935 called *Radical Religion*. Later renamed, *Christianity & Crisis*, the magazine existed until 1994.

He opposed pacifism and helped political organizations supporting the Allies during World War II. Among his efforts was trying to help European Jews escape the Nazis. Considered by many America's leading theologian, Niebuhr was even bruited as a possible candidate for president in 1948.

Other books included *An Interpretation of Christian Ethics, The Irony of American History, The Self & the Dramas of History*, and the two-volume *The Nature & Destiny of Man*.

Niebuhr received many honors, including being made an Honorary Doctor of Divinity by Yale, Harvard and Oxford universities. He died on June 1, 1971 at Stockbridge, Massachusetts.

Among many memorable quotes and lines from his books and sayings:

"God give us the grace to accept with serenity the things that cannot be changed, courage to change the things which should be changed, and the wisdom to know the difference."

"Without the ultra-rational hopes and passions of religion no society will ever have the courage to conquer despair."

"Democracy is finding proximate solutions to imsoluble problems. America worships success, and the only kind of success the average man understands is obvious success."

"Original sin is not an inherited corruption,
but it is an inevitable facet of human existence.
It is there in every moment of existence, but it has no history."

"The misery of man is derived from his idolatry,
from his partly conscious and partly unconscious efforts to make himself,
his race, and his culture God."

"The quintessence of sin is, in short, that man changes the glory of
the incorruptible God into the image of corruptible man.
He always usurps God's place and claims to be
the final judge of human actions."

"The significance of the law of love is precisely that it is not
just another law, but a law which transcends all law."

"Real religion produces the spirit of humility and repentance.
It destroys moral conceit."

Igor Stravinsky
1882–1971

"Too many pieces of music finish
too long after the end."

One of the giants of the musical world in the 20th century, Igor Stravinsky greatly influenced modern appreciation of ballet and other forms of music during his long and active career, which continued well after he was 65. Born in Oranienbaum near St. Petersburg in Russia, he was substantially affected by his many years in the United States. During his lifetime he was often considered "the world's greatest living composer."

Stravinsky was particularly noted for the sheer energy and boldness invested in his compositions, which often used Russian folk melodies. He was taught by the equally famous composer Nikolai Rimsky-Korsakov.

Stravinsky continued working well after he was 65. He suffered his first stroke in 1956, but remained active and productive for virtually the rest of his life, though needing frequent medical attention and medications. In 1962, when he reached 80, he gave concerts in Los Angeles, Seattle, Toronto, Hamburg, Tel Aviv, Rome, Johannesburg, and other cities. He completed his last work, the *Requiem Canticles,* in 1966 at the age of 84. His last recording session took place in 1967, with his final concert later in 1967.

His post-World War II works include *Orpheus* in 1947; *Mass in G,* 1948; *Cantata,* 1951–52; *Septet,* 1952–53; *Agon,* 1957; *Threni,* 1957–58; *Epitaphium,* 1958–59; *Abraham and Isaac,* 1962–63; and *Introitus: T.S. Eliot in Memoriam* in 1965.

His *Symphony in C,* one of his major compositions, was finished in the U.S. and received its first performance in Chicago in 1940. His *Ebony Concerto,* a special composition for clarinetist Woody Herman and his Band that involved his use of the jazz form, was created in 1945. The *Symphony in Three Movements,* started and finished during World War II, was his first major work solely created in the U.S. *The Rake's Progress,* another major opera, received its world premiere in Venice in 1951 when Stravinsky was 69.

Stravinsky was set to work on another opera with the Welsh poet Dylan Thomas, but Thomas died before they could begin. Instead, Stravinsky composed a piece, *Memoriam Dylan Thomas.* The *Canticum Sacrum* ballet score, commemorating his 75th birthday, was performed in 1957. In 1962, when he reached 80, three new compositions emerged: *A Sermon, a Narrative, and a Prayer;* a musical play, *The Flood;* and a revised work, *The Five Fingers.*

A lengthy 1962 tour of major cities throughout the world brought him back to the Soviet Union (Russia) for an emotional visit after an absence of 48 years. In his writings, Stravinsky lamented, "The greatest single crisis of my life as a composer was the loss of Russia, and its language not only of music but of words."

Stravinsky leapt into fame in 1910 when he was invited to compose material for the Ballets Russe for the upcoming season at the Paris Opera. *The Firebird* created substantial interest, as did his next work, *Petrushka,* in 1911. The greatest excitement, however, came in 1913 with the world premiere of his epochal *The Rite of Spring,* whose innovative tonal language and exuberant orchestration ushered in a new era of modernism in music. Noted composer Camille Saint-Saens even left the theater in disapproval, and there were said to be fights that broke out in the audience.

Working in the neoclassical style, Stravinsky in following years created such works as the *Symphony of Psalms* in 1930, *Concerto in D for Violin and Orchestra,* 1931, and *Credo,* 1932.

Stravinsky became a French citizen in 1934, but with World War II looming he came to the United States. After teaching in 1939–1940 at Harvard he settled in Los Angeles and promptly filed his naturalization papers. He also planted beets in his garden for use in making borscht. After a visit to movie studios he described them as "separate principalities."

Concerned over the turbulent world situation, and where an essentially non-political artist could work, he once asked a friend if a revolution was imminent or possible in the U.S. When told it was feasible, he said, "But where will I go?"

Fortunately, Stravinsky was able to compose in peace, and in 1945 he became an American citizen. In Hollywood he began to write scores for films while continuing other compositions. While he was fond of movies, he was less than enchanted, however, with the use of his *Sacre du Printemps* in Disney's film *Fantasia*. After attending some Hollywood parties, he and his wife Catherine (he married in 1906) were said to resort to reading classic novels by such authors as Dostoevsky and Tolstoy to restore their faith in human beings.

Not always a fan of critics, Stravinsky once opined, "I never understand what exactly are the critics complaining about when criticizing my music. But where is the guarantee that their judgment, or opinion, is a professional one? And, after all, are they so important in the history of musical creation?"

Stravinsky recognized changing musical patterns, writing when he was 75 that he should "try to discover whatever new thing it is that makes the new generation new."

His book *The Politics of Music* came out in 1947, when he turned 65. A revised edition of his two volume *Chronicle of My Life* was published in 1972. Several books were written with a collaborator, Robert Craft, including *Conversations with Igor Stravinsky,* 1959; *Memories and Commentaries,* 1960; *Expositions and Developments,* 1960; and *Dialogue and a Diary,* 1963.

Much lauded for his many contributions to music, Stravinsky died in 1971 at the age of 89.

My music is best understood by children and animals."

"Sins cannot be undone, only forgiven."

"In order to creare there must be a dynamic force, and what force is more potent than love?"

"Music's exclusive function is to structure the flow of time and keep order in it."

My God, so much I like to drink Scotch that sometimes I think my name is Igor Stra-whiskey."

Pablo Picasso
1881–1973

"Every child is an artist.
The problem is how to remain an artist once he grows up."

No artist in history had as large a following and audience in his career as Pablo Picasso. He created an immense number of works of art (22,000) in various media including paintings, drawings, etchings, sculpture, ceramics and mosaics. Many of his works were created during the latter decades of his long life, well after he was 65.

Picasso was born in Malaga, Spain on Oct. 25, 1881. He attended the Royal Academy of Art in Barcelona at the tender age of 15, won a prize for painting at 16, and soon decamped to the art world of Paris. His career went through some notable and overlapping color-coded stages. His so-called Blue Period, around 1901–1904, featured many works with blue a dominant color, reflecting to some extent his reaction to the poor workers he saw as well as the suicide of a friend. His subsequent Rose Period saw lighter colors suffusing his paintings.

Late in 1906 an entirely new period emerged, one that changed the course of the art world. Along with others, Picasso was instrumental in the movement away from purely representational art to the concept of Cubism, which rearranged practical space along more geometrical terms. Form and matter were rearranged in striking images, with the artist painting things from different angles as sharply separate items. By 1910 the revolutionary movement had coalesced to deconstructing objects into their parts with the goal of presenting a concept of the thing instead of the natural perception. This led in turn to what was called "Synthetic Cubism," which had oil elements pasted onto canvases, as in collages. Picasso also used cloth and paper to make collages of various kinds, including sculptural ones.

In between the world wars Picasso's fame grew until he became the best known artist in the world. His most famous painting of this period was easily *Guernica* (1937), a stirring portrayal of the savage bombing of that town during the Spanish Civil War.

Picasso continued to live in Paris during the German occupation of World War II. Though the Nazis considered his work to be "degenerate," his fame protected him. After the war, his repute continued to serve him well, though other artists were disgraced by any perception of their affiliation or association with or acceptance of fascism. His endorsement of Stalin after World War II also failed to generate much criticism, with his role as a great artist remaining paramount.

In 1944 Picasso joined the French Communist Party, apparently believing it represented such values as social justice and equal opportunity. But Picasso's 1953 magazine cover drawing of Stalin after his death was deemed short of "social realism," and Picasso felt into disfavor with the party. The feeling was somewhat mutual by this time. He did receive two Lenin Peace Prizes in 1950 and 1962.

Always innovative, Picasso had the first exhibit of his pottery in Paris in 1948. In 1949 he designed a dove for a Peace Congress that ultimately became a worldwide symbol of peace. He also started decorating plates, glasses and vases.

In 1952, at the age of 71, he began the "Temple of Peace" project at the Vallauris Chapel at Vallauris, France, with murals depicting Peace and War. Picasso also completed a play (his second), *Les Quatre Petite Filles (The Four Little Girls),* which was produced to less than enthusiastic acclaim.

La Mystere Picasso, a film covering his work, came out in 1955.

The year 1963 brought a signal honor with the opening of the Picasso Museum in Barcelona. Not to be outdone, though a couple of decades had elapsed, Paris opened its own Picasso Museum in 1985. In 1967 Picasso turned down the Legion of Honor from the French government.

In the last two decades of his life Picasso produced more work than at any other time of his life—as many as eight creations a day. He also commanded high prices for his work. During this period he noted the creation of some his works by not only the year, month and day, but also by Roman numeral to indicate multiple works created that day. This stage of his life contains some of his finest works, such as *L'Aubade, Man with Nude Woman, Man with Pipe, Musketeer, Rembrandtesque Figure and Cupid, Le Cirque* and *Matador and Nude Woman.* He also created a mural commissioned for the UNESCO Building in Paris.

In response to questions about his dating works, Picasso explained, "Why do you think I date everything I do? Because it is not sufficient to know an artistic work. It is also necessary to know when he did them, why, how, under what circumstances? Some day there will undoubtedly be a science—it may be called the science of man—which will seek to know more about man in general through the study of the creative man. I often think about such a science, and I want to leave to posterity a documentation that will be as complete as possible. That's why I put a day on everything I do."

At the age of 87 Picasso, despite failing eyesight (as well as hearing), produced 347 engravings. Working feverishly, he finished as many as seven plates in a single day. Some of this work showed his acknowledgement of his advanced age, while continuing his sensual approach to the female figure. Erotic images, some imbued with humor, were other highlights.

In his personal life Picasso was considered to be moody and difficult but often charming. Being a parent was not considered one of his many talents. The women in his life were the subjects of many of his works. In particular, the face of Jacqueline Rogue—whom he married in 1961, when he was 80—is represented in some fashion in many of his paintings and engravings. Then there was his famous, or infamous, quote of women being either "goddesses or doormats."

His 80th birthday was celebrated throughout the world. At the age of 92, Picasso died in 1973 in his house at Notre-Dame-de-Vie and was buried at the Chateau de Vauvenargues. But his works live on.

Among other quotes:

"Others talk. I work."

"Everything approaches on its own, including death."

"Ultimately, there is only love."

"It's your work in life that is the ultimate seduction."

David Ben-Gurion
1886–1973

"The difficult we do immediately.
The impossible takes a little longer."

David Ben-Gurion is revered as the "George Washington of Israel" and "Father of the Nation," among other expressions, having served as a leading founder of a new country that greatly affected world and Middle East history. He was the first prime minister of Israel, directing the fledgling nation first in 1948, when the country achieved independence, through 1953, and then again in 1955–1963 when he had already passed 65 and required an increasing amount of medical care.

Ben-Gurion retired from political life in 1970 very much the living symbol of Israeli/Jewish spirit and courage. He was voted one of the top 100 people who shaped the 20th century by *Time* magazine.

Ben-Gurion was born David Gruen in Plonsk, Poland when the area was part of Russia. By his mid-teens (he began studying Hebrew at the age of three) he had become a fervent Zionist, seeking a homeland for the world's Jews, ideally a Jewish state in Palestine, where the Jews had lived in ancient times before the Diaspora (the scattering of Jews after exile to Babylonia). "From my tenth year on, I never thought of spending my life anywhere else," he later wrote.

His subsequent activities included leading "Ezra," a Zionist youth group that only spoke Hebrew among themselves. Appalled by the pogroms against Jews in Russia, he went to Palestine in 1906 "to build and to be rebuilt by it," as the motto of the times went. The Ottoman Empire (later to become Turkey) controlled the region during this period. He worked on a farm—his first job was removing manure—and continued his activities as a secular Jewish nationalist seeking a biblical homeland for Jewry.

Of this period he later wrote: "…the settlement of the land is the only true Zionism, all else being self-deception, empty verbiage and merely a hobby." In another significant statement, he opined, "The true right to a country—as to anything else——springs not from political or court authority, but from work."

As for work on the land, he also said, "It is true that the Lord did not put soil on all the rocks, but that was because He wanted us to have the satisfaction of putting it there ourselves."

While World War I raged he fought with the British forces against the Turks. He also was involved in formation of the first workers' commune, which evolved into a kibbutz, a communal farm/settlement, and "The Watchmen," a Jewish self-defense group. As a journalist in Jerusalem in 1910, editing a Hebrew-language newspaper, he first used the persona of Ben-Gurion ("young lion" in Hebrew) as it was relatively close to his real name.

During World War I he also helped form the Jewish Legion, which fought in support of the British. He was deported by the Ottoman authorities to Cairo. But he wound up in New York, where he taught himself English, worked to generate immigration of young Jews to Palestine, and developed an appreciation of American-style democracy. He also met and married his wife, Paula, a Russian nurse and fellow activist—though her zeal was less than his—in 1917. They had three children in a marriage of over 50 years.

While the war was still underway the famed Balfour Declaration promised a homeland for the Jews. Unknown to Ben-Gurion and others, the British managed to also tell the Arabs that Palestine would be theirs. Subsequently, the newly formed League of Nations designated Palestine as a "National Homeland" for the Jewish people.

After the war, with the British now in control of Palestine, Ben-Gurion had the vision to realize that both Jews and Arabs wanted to possess the same land. He realized that the Arabs were increasingly unhappy over growing Jewish immigration to Palestine and purchase of land, and that eventually the resettled Jews would need military strength to survive. Accordingly, he helped create the *Histradrut,* the Jewish labor federation, and served as its leader for 14 years. The organization evolved into the Labor Party, which later governed Israel for three decades after independence in 1948.

Ben-Gurion also served as chairman of the Zionist Executive and the Jewish Agency for Palestine from 1935. In a 1939 "White Paper," England effectively abrogated its Balfour Declaration (which had been mostly symbolic), and limited Jewish immigration to Palestine, a much desired move by the Arabs; however, the controversial decision unleashed even greater Jewish determination to secure a homeland.

During World War II Ben-Gurion counseled, "We must support the British in this war as if there was no White Paper, and fight the White Paper as if there was no war." He helped organize an underground agency to smuggle Jews fleeing the Nazis in Europe into Palestine.

After the end of the war the situation was tense in Palestine, with Jewish immigration still limited. Great Britain, desirous of maintaining its oil supply, supported the Arabs. Ben-Gurion continued to lead the struggle, authorizing acts of sabotage against the English and the amassment of arms for the conflict he expected to break out.

Finally the United Nations voted to partition Palestine between Jews and Arabs, finding they both had valid but irreconcilable claims to the same land. The Jews accepted this decision; the Arabs didn't. The independent state of Israel was declared on May 14, 1948, with Ben-Gurion as the new nation's provisional leader. Under his forceful leadership (he became a quick study in military tactics and strategy), the Israelis managed to defeat the joint Arab forces representing five countries.

Ben-Gurion guided the development of Israel, including pioneer farm/settlements, rural development projects, creating new towns and cities, and airlifting Jews from Arab countries to Israel in the famed "Operation Red Carpet." He also advocated using Hebrew as the language of Israel. While not religious, he also pushed for the Sabbath being on Saturday and not Sunday to preserve Jewish tradition. In effect, he had to give religious leaders some of their desires in order to secure a working political coalition, and especially to handle national defense and foreign affairs.

"The Law of Return," which permitted Jews from around the world the right to immigrate to Israel, was passed. In five years the Israeli population virtually doubled. In a controversial decision he persuaded the Knesset, the Israeli parliament, to accept reparations from West Germany in 1952. His policy of reprisals against Arab attacks was criticized by some as contributing to the cycle of violence between the two sides.

Ben-Gurion served as prime minister until late 1953, when he moved to the Sder Boker ("Field of the Horseman") kibbutz in the Negev desert, where he lived in a one-story, four-room prefabricated house that still had the usual modern conveniences—including a library. While he was willing to do manual labor, he was assigned the task of feeding newborn lambs.

He returned to power as Prime Minister in 1955 to again lead Israel during the 1956 Suez Canal campaign. In 1957 he survived an assassination attempt by a deranged Israeli. Once more he resigned in 1963, but remained a member of the Knesset.

After the 1967 war with the Arab states, a conflict he opposed while displaying less aggressiveness than in his earlier days, he argued against Israel holding on to conquered Arab territory.

In 1970, at the age of 84, he retired from political life and returned to the kibbutz to work on his memoirs and a history of Israel. In 1971 a special session of the Knesset honored him on his 85th birthday, declaring his birthday a national holiday. He died in 1973 about two months after the end of yet another war with the Arabs, the Yom Kippur war.

On his tomb near a Mosaic site not far from the kibbutz he asked for an inscription of "The Old Man" (as he was fondly called) and a citation that he came to Palestine/Israel in 1906—which he considered the most important event of his life. He was buried next to his wife, who had predeceased him in 1968.

Among his books, all written after he was 65, are *Rebirth and Destiny of Israel* in 1954, *Israel: Years of Challenge* in 1965, *Israel's Security* in 1960, *Israel: A Personal History* and *Memoirs* in 1970, and *My Talks with Arabs* in 1973. *The Jews in Their Land* was published posthumously in 1974.

In addition to the Ben-Gurion Airport at Tel Aviv, there is a Ben-Gurion University of the Negev, a Ben-Gurion Institute to study his life and achievements, and his home in Tel-Aviv houses a museum.

Among his many memorable comments:

"In Israel, in order to be a realist, you must believe in miracles."

*"Without moral and intellectual independence,
there is no anchor for national independence."*

*"The State of Israel will prove itself not by material wealth,
not by military might or technical achievement,
but by its moral character and human values."*

*"It matters not what the Gentiles will say,
but what the Jews will do."*

*"Anyone who believes you can't change history
has never tried to write his memoirs."*

"If an expert says it can't be done, get another expert."

*"Courage is a special kind of knowledge:
the knowledge of how to fear what ought to be feared
and how not to fear what ought not to be feared."*

Casey Stengel
1891–1975

"All right, everybody line up alphabetically according to your height."

Not many people have a kind of "language" named after them, but Casey Stengel—the famed Major League baseball manager—achieved this signal honor by sportswriters struck by his disconnected, stream-of-consciousness double-talk on various subjects, not just baseball. His monologues and malapropisms were dubbed "Stengelese," and Stengel acquired the fond nickname of the "Old Perfessor."

Stengel spent 54 years in baseball, both as a player and a manager. He managed until he was 73, and many of his most successful years as a manager came after he was 65.

Stengel was born in Kansas City in 1890 as Charles Dillon Stengel. His nickname of "Casey" came from KC, the city of his birth. He studied dentistry for a while but then settled on baseball, a career that dominated the rest of his life. He married his wife, Edna, in 1924.

Early on, Stengel demonstrated his comic touch. At one Minor League game he found a manhole in the outfield he played. He lowered himself into the manhole and then emerged to catch a fly ball—to the surprise of fans and probably some players, too. On another occasion he brought a flashlight onto the field in an attempt to convince the umpires it had become too dark to keep playing a game. He was one of the first, if not the first, player to wear sunglasses while in the field. Once, when coaching, he held an open umbrella to protest a game being continued in the rain.

The most famous incident came about in 1919 in a game between the Brooklyn Dodgers, his former team, and the Pittsburgh Pirates, his current team. As the story goes, he somehow received a sparrow from a Dodger pitcher in the bullpen (where pitchers warmed up before entering a game) and put it under his cap. After being booed by Dodger fans, displeased by his having changed teams, he doffed his cap to release the bird when he stood at the plate about to hit. The fans were both astonished and appreciative, as shown by their cheering and clapping.

While sometimes clowning around, Stengel was still shrewd as a baseball tactician and in his business investments as well. Edna, his wife of over 50 years, generally took care of the business end, and very successfully, as his varied interests made him a millionaire.

Stengel's Major League playing career ended in 1925 after he had played in three World Series, helping to win several games with dramatic base hits.

After managing some teams in the Minor Leagues, he returned to the Major Leagues and managed the then Boston Braves. Antics continued, including bringing a railroad lantern to the field when the umpires refused to stop a game, which the Braves were losing, in growing darkness; and donning a raincoat and galoshes and carrying an umbrella when the umpires didn't want to stop or call a game because of rain.

Despite Stengel's somewhat dubious reputation for seriousness—though not his knowledge of the game—he was chosen to become manager of the very serious New York Yankees, for whom winning was an imperative. He led the Yankees to a remarkable 10 pennants in 12 years during the 1949–1960 period, during which he turned 65. This tenure was marked even more by a record-making five consecutive World Series triumphs 1949–1953.

While his skills as a manager were recognized, and the fans and media reveled in his comments, not all of his players always appreciated his motivational techniques. Stengel was also a great proponent of platooning players, inserting hitters who batted from the right side of the plate against left-handed pitchers and vice versa. His last year of managing the Yankees, in 1960, was considered one of his best, given injuries to players and other factors, even though the team lost the World Series.

Stengel also entertained the U.S. Senate with his odd attack on the English language during 1958 hearings before the Senate Subcommittee on Antitrust and Monopoly.

Despite health problems, some probably due to his drinking, he continued managing and winning. After a hospital examination, he quipped, "They examined all my organs. Some of them are quite remarkable and others are not so good. A lot of museums are bidding for them." Soon after turning 70 he said, "Most people my age are dead at the present time, and you can look it up."

But after the 1960 season, in his seventh decade, the Yankees let him go. Stengel's reaction was, "They told me my services were no longer desired because they wanted to put in a youth program as an advance way of keeping the club going. I'll never make the mistake of being 70 again."

Undaunted, Stengel took on the challenge of managing the New York Mets (1962–65), a much inferior team that was ridiculed at times. Even Stengel said, "Can't anybody here play the game?"

However, while the Mets lost many games on the field, their play and record—coupled with his colorful commentary—did bring the team considerable sympathy and popularity. Stengel continued at the team's helm even after suffering fractured hips; he finally got an artificial hip at the age of 75. After the 1965 season, Stengel finally retired at the age of 73.

He lived another 10 years, continuing to do some exercises in the morning and a bit of drinking and smoking later on in the day. His autobiography, *Casey At The Bat,* came out in 1962. He was elected into the Baseball Hall of Fame in 1966.

Death came at the age of 86 in Glendale, California. A plaque at his grave, befitting his distinctive life and language, reads: "There comes a time in every man's life, and I've had many of them."

Among many quotes by Stengel:

"Never make predictions, especially about the future."

"If people don't want to come to the ballpark, nobody can stop them."

"They're very much alike in a lot of similarities."

"The trick is growing up without growing old."

"Managing is getting paid for homeruns someone else hits."

"I want to thank all my players for giving me the honor of being what I was."

"Being with a woman all night never hurt no professional baseball players. It's staying up all night looking for a woman that does harm."

"The secret of managing is to keep the guys who hate you away from the guys who are undecided."

"If anyone wants me, tell them I'm being embalmed."

"It's wonderful to meet so many friends that I didn't use to like."

And befitting his distinctive speaking style, Stengel responded when asked why he had never visited Montreal:

"Because then there'd be two languages I couldn't speak—French and English."

Charles Chaplin
1889–1977

"A day without laughter is a day wasted."

Charles Chaplin was an extremely talented comic actor, as well as a director and writer, whose many contributions to filmmaking continues to greatly affect the art form. In a worldwide survey of movie critics in 1955 Chaplin was voted the greatest actor in film history.

Two of his many movies—*A King in New York* in 1957 and *A Countess from Hong Kong* in 1967—both came out after he was 65. The former film was his last in a starring role. His life's story, *My Autobiography,* was published in 1964 when he was 75.

Chaplin was born in 1889. His parents were music hall performers in London, and he began his show business career in theaters at the tender age of five. Starting as a dancer, he worked his way up to acting. When he was on a tour with a theater company in the U.S. in 1912 his talent was recognized by the head of Keystone Studios in Los Angeles, which signed him to a contract the next year. Upon arrival in New York for the first time he was supposed to have said, "I give you fair warning, America! I'm coming to conquer you."

Chaplin, confident over his talent, began developing his famed "Tramp" persona and made his mark with slapstick that still conveyed subtlety in character. In discussing the complexities of developing and acting his comic character, Chaplin once revealed, "It's a desperate business being a clown."

He made 35 movies for Keystone, including writing and directing among the latter films, before moving on to another movie studio. In 1916, while with still another studio, he made two noted comedies, *The Immigrant* and *Easy Street.* He was criticized for not being a soldier during World War I, but Army doctors were said to have rejected him.

However, his Tramp character had struck a chord with the public and he was quite popular, with his name even bandied about in songs and ditties. He continued working, with his fan base increasing as well. *The Immigrant,* Chaplin commented, affected him the most of any of his films.

Another major film, *The Kid,* helped catapult him into international fame and enormous financial rewards (as much as $10,000 a week). He was easily one of the most significant cinematic artists of the silent film era. By 1920 "Chaplinitis" led to the creation of various dances, songs, dolls, comic books and cocktails that used his persona in some fashion.

Chaplin became the first actor to gain control of the production and distribution ends of the movie business when he—along with Mary Pickford, Douglas Fairbanks, Sr., and D.W. Griffith—created United Artists, a process started in 1918. Moreover, Chaplin was involved in casting, scoring and editing to addition to acting, writing and directing. He was noted for his great attention to detail and for shooting many takes of a scene until he was satisfied.

The Gold Rush, another memorable film, came out in 1925, followed by *City Lights* in 1931. Chaplin was slow to adapt to the sound era, but his success continued with *Modern Times* in 1936. *The Great Dictator,* a spoof on Hitler, appeared in 1940. In reacting to the sea change in films through the use of sound, Chaplin noted that before the advent of sound "actors had grasped an alphabet of gesture, the poetry of movement. They know that gesture begins where words leave off." Nevertheless, he skillfully navigated into the new era of filmmaking.

His personal life was somewhat troubled, marked by a pattern of his being attracted to very young girls. He married 15-year-old Mildred Harris, a film extra, in 1917, with the union lasting two years. Next came 16-year-old Lita Gray in 1924, with the marriage bringing a tough-minded and show-business savvy mother-in-law. This marriage led to a bitter and costly divorce. Paulette Goddard, at 19, became his next bride, with the marriage lasting nine years. In 1943, when 54, he married 18-year-old Oona O'Neill, daughter of the famed playwright Eugene O'Neill, who was less than thrilled by the match.

During World War II Chaplin was beset by a paternity suit lodged by actress Joan Barry and accusations of being an anti-American pacifist and a security risk. Chaplin paid taxes in the U.S., but remained a British subject his entire life; the fact that he hadn't become an American citizen didn't help his cause. The FBI accumulated a sizeable file, and he was eventually charged with violation of the Mann Act (transporting a woman across state lines for illegal sexual purposes) and Barry's civil rights. Federal charges over the Mann Act were finally dropped, and a blood test eventually proved he wasn't the father of Barry's child. But California, which didn't use blood tests as evidence at that time, ruled in a second trial in 1945 that Chaplin was the father of the then two-year-old boy and that he had to pay child support until the child was 18.

Monsieur Verdoux, a black comedy, was produced in 1947. But it was *Limelight,* one of Chaplin's greatest films, which came out in 1952, that drew substantial acclaim. Chaplin took his family to London for the English premiere of the movie. Unfortunately, to reenter the country (this was during the McCarthy period), he had to pass muster with U.S. Immigration and Naturalization. Chaplin refused to submit to what he considered a humiliation, and he went into voluntary exile in 1953.

In 1972 Chaplin received an honorary Oscar "for the incalculable effect he has had in making motion pictures the art form of the century." In 1973, somewhat belatedly, he received another Oscar for his score for *Limelight.* He was knighted by Queen Elizabeth in 1975.

Death came at his Swiss villa at Vesey (where he had also received the controversial medical treatment of transplantation of cells from sheep fetuses to replace or revitalize waning organs) in 1977.

In 1981, in a fitting tribute, a statue of Chaplin (a replica of a statue in Vevey) was unveiled in London's Leicester Square close to a statue of another great artist, Shakespeare. One of the more signal honors for his "Tramp" character came when IBM used this highly recognizable figure as the logo in advertising its entry into the personal computer field in the 1980s.

Chaplin, who could be self-critical, once said of himself, "I'm an emotional cuss." Among his other pithy comments were:

"Failure is unimportant. It takes courage to make a fool of oneself."

"Nothing is permanent in this wicked world—not even our troubles."

"All I need to make a comedy is a park, a policeman and a pretty girl."

"I went into the business for the money, and the art grew out of it. If people are disillusioned by that remark, I can't help it. It's the truth."

"I don't believe the public knows what it wants; this is the conclusion I have drawn from my career."

"Life is a tragedy when seen in close-up, but a comedy in long-shot."

"The saddest thing I can imagine is to get used to luxury."

Margaret Mead
1901–1978

"A knowledge of other cultures should
sharpen our ability to scrutinize more steadily,
to appreciate more lovingly,
our own."

"I have spent most of my life
studying the lives of other peoples—
faraway peoples—
so that Americans
might better understand themselves."

These comments reflect the enormous impact Margaret Mead, hailed as one of the foremost anthropologists of the 20th century, had in helping to popularize anthropology and its cultural implications to the American public. Over her long life she wrote 44 books and over a thousand articles. She headed as president many organizations in the science/culture fields, lectured extensively, and testified often on social issues before Congress and various government agencies.

Several of her books were written after she was 65, including *Culture and Commitment: A Study of the Generation Gap,* 1970, *Blackberry Winter,* 1972, and *Letters from the Field, 1925–1975,* 1977. After her last field trip to conduct major research, in 1953, she spent the remainder of her life writing and making many speaking engagements.

Mead is best known for her 1928 book, *Coming of Age in Samoa,* in which she explored the cultural influences on sexual behavior among adolescents. She had begun field work in Samoa in 1925 when she was hardly 23. The book contended that culture more than biology affected the amount of stress felt by adolescent young women. While becoming a bestseller, her book also elicited negative comments about its candid sexual content; one state governor even referred to Mead as a "dirty old lady."

Other major books included *Growing Up in New Guinea,* 1930,

Sex and Temperament in Three Primitive Societies, 1935, *Male and Female: A Study of the Sexes in a Changing World,* 1949, *New Lives for Old: Cultural Transformation—Manus, 1928–1953,* 1956, *Continuities in Cultural Evolution,* 1964, and *Anthropologists and What They Do,* 1965. Another key work was *And Keep Your Powder Dry: An Anthropologist Looks at America,* which came out in 1942.

In discussing field work, Mead said, "The way to do field work is never to come up for air until it is all over." She also commented about "the open-mindedness with which one must look and listen."

Mead was the first anthropologist to study child-rearing practices, and her work helped to establish links between anthropology and other fields. Her interests varied greatly, including writings about mental and spiritual health, education, ecology, ethics, overpopulation and nuclear bombs. While she didn't consider herself a feminist per se, she also contributed material on women's issues. Before photography became as commonplace as it is now, she wove the use of photos into her research and writings.

Never reluctant to express an opinion, or risk what might be an unpopular opinion, she was even said to have proposed to pay students to go to college, and to sanction trial student marriages. Another modest suggestion, made in 1961, was that couples should spend the first two weeks of their honeymoon in a bomb shelter to help assure that any babies conceived during this time period would be safe from nuclear radiation and thus be able to sustain mankind. In this latter vein, she also opined, "It's nonsense to talk about a third world war as if a fourth would follow."

Mead argued that marriages shouldn't be expected to always last a lifetime. On the issue of marijuana, she told a Senate subcommittee that prohibition could create more problems than any overuse.

The notoriety of the subjects she spoke out about led to some ditties such as:

> *Margaret Mead, Margaret Mead*
> *Helps to fill our country's need,*
> *Thinks our culture is much lower*
> *Than the one that's in Samoa*

She wrote a monthly column for *Redbook* magazine. In addition, she served as president of the Society for Applied Anthropology, the World Federation of Mental Health, and the American Anthropological Association. She was the first woman to be president of the American Association for the Advancement of Science. She served during part of World War II as executive secretary of the National Research Council's Committee of Food Habits in Washington, D.C.

In 1942 she received the first gold medal issued by the Society of Woman Geographers. In a 1941 speech emphasizing the role of social science, "Spontaneity as a Condition of Democratic Life," she advocated that the growing use of propaganda be utilized "to influence the behavior of human beings to use the laws developed by social scientists instead of the intuitions of natural politicians."

When she was 75, the American Association for the Advancement of Science held a celebration in her honor. At one reception she quipped, "I expect to die, but I don't plan to retire."

Mead, who was born in Philadelphia, received her Ph.D. from Columbia University. She served as a member of the curatorial staff of the American Museum of Natural History in New York City from 1926 until her death. She was also a professor of anthropology at Columbia University after 1954.

Death came in New York at the age of 78. She received the Presidential Medal of Freedom posthumously. The Library of Congress has her many writings in its archives.

Among her many memorable comments:

"Always remember that you are absolutely unique. Just like everyone else."

"Thanks to television, for the first time the young are seeing history made before it is censored by their elders."

"Of all the peoples whom I have studied, from city dwellers to cliff dwellers, I always find that at least 50 percent would prefer to have at least one jungle between themselves and their mothers-in-law."

"Life in the 20th century is like a parachute jump— you have to get it right the first time."

"I learned the virtue of hard work by hard work."

"Never doubt that a small group of thoughtful,
committed citizens can change the world.
Indeed, it is the only thing that has."

"What people say, what people do, and what they say they do
are entirely different things."

"Everytime we liberate a woman, we liberate a man."

"One of the oldest human needs is having someone wonder where you are
when you don't come home at night."

Marc Chagall
1887–1985

"Great art picks up where nature ends."

Considered one of the most original and distinctive painters of the 20th century, Marc Chagall was also a master lithographer, printmaker and designer. He continued creating works of art well past his 65th birthday, though burdened by the growing infirmities of old age as well as the turbulence of the 20th century's hot and cold wars. Imaginatively blending Jewish folklore and Russian customs/traditions, his paintings tended to stir deep feelings of a mysterious form of reality in viewers while serving as a vivid but non-representational pictorial biography of sorts.

Among his great works accomplished after he was 65 were the magnificent 12 stained glass windows reflecting the 12 tribes of Israel that he created for the synagogue of the Hadassah-Hebrew University Medical Center in Jerusalem when he was a mere 75. In 1964 he completed the ceiling panorama atop the Paris Opera, which involved painting over 2,300 square feet. At the age of 77 he had to ascend some 75 feet of scaffolding to reach the ceiling (his work had been glued to polyester panels at the ceiling) to attend to touching up details. He was also given an exhibit at the Louvre Museum, the first such honor given a living artist.

Two large mural paintings were also done for the Metropolitan Opera House at Lincoln Center in New York in 1966 when he was 79. Sets and costumes for the Met's 1967 production of Mozart's *Magic Flute* were another of his major accomplishments. Commissions poured in, including the Assy Baptistery in 1957 and the cathedrals of Metz (1960) and Rheims (1974).

He completed a stained glass window for the Chicester Cathedral in West Sussex, England when he was 90.

Age was clearly not a deterrent to being productive and creative. His works are exhibited in many museums around the world, and are often depicted on posters and greeting cards.

Born as Moeshe Segal near Vitebsk, Russia (in what is now Belarus but was then the "Pale of Settlement" where Russian Jews lived) on July 7, 1887, Chagall grew up in a ghetto-like area. His parents were members of a Hasidic sect whose religious tenets and practices—some perhaps an escape from the constraints and discrimination of life in Russia for Jews—greatly influenced him and his future works. Meetings of the sect, where there was dancing and singing as a celebration of life, generated in Chagall a mystical sense in which angels and other creatures, human and otherwise, weren't limited by Earth's gravity. Recalling his younger days, Chagall wrote, "The ceiling suddenly opens and a winged creature descends with a great commotion, a swish of fluttering wings. I think an angel. I can't open my eyes…it is too bright, too luminous."

At the age of 20, encouraged by his mother to cultivate his artistic leanings, he left home to attend the Imperial School of Fine Arts in St. Petersburg. Poverty led to few good meals and some nights spent on park benches. Feeling somewhat constrained by this traditional school, Chagall began attending classes of Leon Bakst, a well-known theatrical designer. Inspired by a feeling of artistic liberation, some of his earlier paintings, such as *Death* in 1908 and *Birth* in 1909, began to draw attention.

Lining up the help of a well-to-do patron, he managed to travel to and study in Paris during the 1910–1914 period. This was a heady time in the French capital, with many personalities, later to be famous artists and writers, sharing ideas and creating works that have withstood the tests of time. Among these luminaries were Picasso, Matisse, Apollinaire, Modigliani, Soutine, and others. During this time he changed his name to Marc Chagall.

Living in the artist area of La Ruche ("the Beehive"), Chagall had Modigliani and Soutine as neighbors. While his technical skill kept maturing, Chagall maintained his own sense of mysterious reality, though other schools of painting—such as Cubism—did provide influence by further freeing his subjects from realistic shapes and movements (including the force of gravity). Cubism showed subjects from many angles, not necessarily realistic, instead of one single and relatively realistic viewpoint; objects might be separated with fragments then placed in unfamiliar-looking constructions. The work of the Fauvists encouraged him to employ vivid colors. "I have brought my subjects from Russia and Paris has given them light," Chagall commented.

Some of his famed works from this period were *In My Village* in 1911, *The Fiddler* in 1912, and *Paris Through My Window* in 1913. His first one-man show came in Berlin in 1914.

Caught in Vitebsk, where he had returned for a visit in 1914, by the start of World War I, he wound up staying in Russia through its 1917 revolution and the advent of the Communist control of the country, through 1922. In 1915 he married Bella Rosenfeld, daughter of a wealthy Vitebsk merchant. During the war some of his work entailed drawings of the wounded. After the war he was named commissar of fine arts for Vitebsk in 1917 by the Bolshevik leaders of Russia. He helped set up an art school and a museum, but subsequently resigned after disagreements over such issues as freedom of the artist to paint some subjects not approved by the reigning authorities.

Moving to Moscow, he began painting scenery for the State Jewish Theater, but then he and his wife departed for Paris later in 1922. One of his most famous paintings, *Over Vitebsk,* was created this year.

In between the world wars Chagall created more paintings, including *The Circus* in 1931 and *Lovers with Roosters* in 1933. He also branched out and produced many lithographs, etchings and book illustrations, including Gogol's *Dead Souls,* La Fontaine's *Fables,* and the Bible. He also became a French citizen.

In 1931, an autobiography, *My Life,* was published. Not an artist favored by the Nazis, he had some of his works shown in the "Degenerate Art Exhibit" orchestrated by the German authorities in 1937. All of his works were also removed from German museums. His painting *The White Crucifixion* was a stirring response to Nazi persecutions.

With the French surrender to the Nazis in 1940, Chagall was in Vichy France, the unoccupied part of the defeated country that was still really under German control. He was fortunate to be among some artists who were spirited out of the country in dramatic fashion by crossing the Pyrenees Mountains into Spain. He was helped by the

Guggenheim family, and was one of the first artists in the famous Guggenheim Collection.

Thus he was able to take his family (wife and daughter) to the U.S. At one point he issued a puzzling question as to whether there were "any cows" in the U.S., as if he thought just skyscrapers and monumental structures dotted the American landscape. However, he was said to just be joking about whether someone with a bovine intelligence like him would be admitted to the U.S.

He stayed in the U.S. until 1948. Some of his great works during this period were *The Juggler* in 1943 and *Cockrow* in 1944, the same year that his wife died. Subsequently, he had a long affair with Virginia Haggard.

But his time in the U.S., in which his English didn't fare too well, also led to some innocuous involvements with various left-wing/liberal/peace groups, which generated FBI scrutiny (he *was* from the Soviet Union, where he had held an official post) and the inevitable file.

In 1948 Chagall returned to Paris and then settled in Saint-Paul-de-Vence in sunny southern France. He endured a pair of successful prostate operations in 1950, and was soon back at work. In 1952 he married again, to Valentina Brodsky. He bought a home, La Colline, at Vence in 1966. It featured a large studio and views of the Mediterranean Sea. More great works followed during the post-World War II period, including *Red Roofs* in 1953 and *Girl with Blue Face* in 1960, when he was over 70. He concentrated on stained glass windows and engravings during his latter decades.

A signal honor came in 1973 with the opening of the Chagall Museum in Nice, France, a museum dedicated to his works, especially his *Biblical Message*.

He passed away in Vence on March 28, 1985, at the age of 98.

Chagall's comments include:

"If a symbol should be discovered in a painting of mine, it was not my intention. It is a result I did not seek. It is something that may be found afterwards, and which can be interpreted according to taste."

"The habit of ignoring nature is deeply implanted in our times. This attitude reminds me of people who never look you in the eye; I find them disturbing and always have to look away."

JACK ADLER

"We all know that a good person can be a bad artist.
But no one will ever be a genuine artist unless he is a great human being,
and thus also a good one."

"I work in whatever medium likes me at the moment."

"In our life there is a single color, as on an artist's palette,
which provides the meaning of life and art.
It is the color of love."

"In the arts, as in life, everything is possible
provided it is based on love."

Andres Segovia
1893–1987

*"Among God's creatures two,
the dog and the guitar,*
*have taken all the sizes and all the shapes
in order not to be separated from men."*

Considered the father of the modern classical guitar, Andres Segovia changed the minds of many of his contemporaries who believed the guitar was only fit for tavern-like performances instead of the concert stage. He made the guitar one of the most popular and studied instruments in the world, for both professionals and amateurs. While enriching the lives of music lovers for five decades he also attracted a wide following.

Segovia, who kept performing and teaching others to play the classical guitar even when he was past 90, was born in Linares and raised in Granada, Spain. He was tutored in the piano and violin, but was less than overwhelmed with interest in these instruments. When he heard the guitar, however, his interest perked. At the Granada Musical Institute he persisted in learning how to play the guitar, even to the extent of teaching himself when he felt competent instruction wasn't otherwise available.

Segovia made his public debut in Granada in 1909 when he was 16, and his professional debut in Madrid in 1912. Performances continued in Barcelona in 1916, and then overseas in South America in 1919. His Paris debut in 1924 was extremely successful, and he received international recognition. After his initial concert in the U.S. in 1928 he toured the country regularly.

Segovia also convinced luthiers, makers of stringed musical instruments, to experiment with different woods and guitar designs to improve the amplification of guitars, among other factors. He also began transposing classical masterpieces, such as Bach pieces, for guitar performance. In effect, in showing how these works could be purely and beautifully expressed on the guitar, he expanded the repertoire for the classical guitar as well as the musical boundaries of the concert stage. Moreover, composers began to arrange original pieces for the guitar.

At the outbreak of the Spanish Civil War in 1936, Segovia relocated first to Genoa in Italy and then to Montevideo, capital of Uruguay in South America. He settled in the U.S. in 1943. He didn't return to his native Spain until after World War II.

During his career Segovia made many recordings. He usually practiced five or more hours a day. He was married three times, and widowed twice.

One of his objectives, set early in his life, was to have the guitar both taught and played around the world. He, himself, taught at Santiago de Compostela in Spain and in Siena, Italy, while also visiting other educational institutions to provide instructional performances/classes. As a result of his efforts, many universities, academies and conservatories today include the guitar in their curriculums for musical studies. Owners of stores selling musical instruments surely owe a debt to Segovia, as guitars represent a steady source of sales.

In his *Autobiography of the Years 1893–1920,* which came out in 1983 and just covers that period of his life, Segovia wrote,

> I found the guitar almost at a standstill…and raised it to the loftiest levels of the musical world. Although at one time, the guitar lacked a legitimate or even a useable repertoire, today a surprising number of works have been and continue to be written for it by renowned composers.

He added,

> I, for one, still stand fast at the ramparts, in and out of planes and tours and concert halls, adapting new and old works in my leisure time. And I'll soon be 83. "Hard work," as a sage once said, "is the strong man's means of self destruction."

True to his words, Segovia kept adapting, playing and teaching for many years after he was 65. He died in Madrid in 1987 at the age of 94. In the year of his death, as an example of his music preeminence, the government of Japan indicated that Segovia had influenced more than two million aspiring guitar students and helped develop a guitar industry in the country. Chances are that other countries could produce comparable statistics.

Among Segovia's quotes:

> *"The piano is a monster that screams when you touch its teeth."*

> *"Sometimes one is without the pleasure of playing.*
> *But when the silence of the audience is perfect, we recover that."*

> *"The advice I am giving always to students is above all*
> *to study the music profoundly...music is like the ocean,*
> *and the instruments are little or bigger islands,*
> *very beautiful for the flowers and trees..."*

Irving Berlin
1888–1989

*"Irving Berlin has no place in American music—
he is American music."*

This tribute by fellow musician Jerome Kern sums up the enormous contributions of Berlin, who composed well over a thousand songs, 19 musicals, and the scores of 18 musicals during a prolific career that lasted nearly 60 years and extended well beyond his 65th birthday. Over half of his more than 450 songs became hits. He was probably the most outstanding American songwriter of the 20th century. Though not as sophisticated in his musical skills as some other composers of his time, his songs had a way of touching the heart.

Even when he was nearly 100 years old, having already survived a stroke and needing to have things read to him because of cataracts, he was still considering projects. His last musical was *Mr. President* in 1962, which, unfortunately, was widely considered a flop. To some extent the tastes of the country had changed from Berlin's heyday. He was still going strong when he was 66 in 1954 with the musical *Count Your Blessings.*

Israel Baline (Berlin's original name) was born in 1888 in Mogilyov in Russia and what is now Belarus (at the time known as the Pale of Settlement, a region set aside for Russian Jews). His family moved to New York when he was 10 to escape pogroms against Russian Jews, and settled in a tenement on the Lower East Side. After his father died he took to singing in the street in his new language of English for tips, and then worked as a singing waiter in Bowery saloons.

While he couldn't read music, he managed to teach himself to play the piano well enough to begin writing songs. In 1907 he achieved his first success with the publication of a song, "Marie from Sunny Italy."

In that same year he changed his name to Irving Berlin. "Alexander's Ragtime Band" in 1911 was his first big song hit.

His first musical, *Watch Your Step,* was produced in 1914 and was a major success. By 1919 he was successful enough to establish his own company by which means he could avoid sharing royalties with publishers; and by 1921 he was staging annual reviews at his own Broadway theater, the Music Box, which he created to skip dealing with theater owners.

He wrote patriotic songs during both world wars, starting with the musical *Yip, Yip, Yaphank,* which featured the famed song, "Oh, How I Hate to Get Up in the Morning" (he was drafted into the Army before turning 30, shortly after becoming a citizen in 1918). His most notable song, however, was "God Bless America," which came out on Armistice Day in 1938. The popularity of this song led to some wanting it to replace the national anthem.

World War II, when he traveled with his show, *This is the Army,* brought forth such memorable songs as "This is the Army, Mr. Jones" and "I Left My Heart at the Stage Door Canteen."

Of his patriotic compositions, Berlin commented, "A patriotic song is an emotion and you must not embarrass an audience with it, or they will hate your guts."

Among his many songs were "How Deep is the Ocean," "Cheek to Cheek," "Anything You Can Do, I Can Do Better," "There's No Business Like Show Business," "Easter Parade," "Blue Skies," "Always" and "White Christmas." Two of his most successful musicals were *Annie Get Your Gun* in 1950 and *Call Me Madam* in 1953. His fame was such that his name was routinely listed in front of the title of some musicals, such as *Irving Berlin's On the Avenue, Irving Berlin's This is the Army,* and *Irving Berlin's White Christmas.*

Berlin's song "Blue Skies" was featured in *The Jazz Singer,* the first talkie movie. Subsequently, he wrote scores for such films as *Top Hat, Follow the Fleet* and *On the Avenue.*

Berlin composed his material on a special transposing piano that enabled him to shift keys through a lever, as he remained unable to actually write musical notations. Generally he would either sing or play his material, both music and lyrics, for an assistant to transcribe into musical notations.

Berlin was generous with his success, donating to several charities. Most notably, he turned over all royalties from "God Bless America" to the Boy Scouts and Girl Scouts. He also co-founded ASCAP, the American Society of Composers, Authors & Publishers.

On a personal basis, Berlin's first wife died of typhoid fever only months after their honeymoon. He later eloped at the age of 37 with a well-known socialite who was Catholic, and whose wealthy father so disapproved of the match that he disinherited her. They were married for decades until she passed away. They had three daughters.

Though successful both professionally and financially, Berlin still felt a measure of insecurity, probably stemming from his early days of poverty. At a party, a woman said, "I guess there's no one who has written as many hits as you have."

Berlin's rejoinder: "I know there's no one who has written so many failures."

In his latter years Berlin became more of a recluse and very protective of his copyrights as well as his privacy. He wasn't keen on allowing publication or use of his songs, such as for television commercials. He suffered from depression, which led to his retirement. "I worried about everything when, really, I had nothing to worry about," Berlin admitted. In a related comment, he said, "You can stand success, but you're afraid of failure."

Berlin received many honors, including the Congressional Gold Medal, given by President Dwight D. Eisenhower in 1955 in recognition of his patriotic services and songs. His World War I doughboy uniform and some of his patriotic scores are on exhibit at the Jewish War Veterans Museum in Washington, D.C. There were some accusations of plagiarism due to his tremendous output, but those charges were dismissed.

A centennial celebration of his rags-to-riches and eminently creative life and works was held at Carnegie Hall in New York in 1988. He received a tribute from ASCAP using some of the words from one of his famous songs: "Irving Berlin's music will last for not just an hour, not just for a day, not for just a year, but always."

Berlin died a year later at the age of 101. A number of admirers sang "God Bless America" outside his house on the occasion of his death.

Among his comments:

> *"Everyone ought to have a Lower East Side in their life."*
> (Even when close to being 100,
> Berlin would revisit the Lower East Side
> of his early years in the U.S.)

> *"The toughest thing about success is that you've got to keep on being*
> *a success. Talent is only a starting point in this business.*
> *You've got to keep on working that talent.*
> *Some day I'll reach for it and it won't be there."*

Thurgood Marshall
1908–1993

"I have a lifetime appointment
and I intend to serve it. I expect to die at 110,
shot by a jealous husband."

More than anyone else, probably, Thurgood Marshall is responsible for the improvement of civil rights for all Americans, especially African Americans. In successfully convincing the Supreme Court as an attorney for the National Association for the Advancement of Colored People (NAACP) to overturn the "separate but equal" doctrine, he achieved an end to segregation in public schools. His overriding ambition was to foster complete integration, which he felt was the only way to insure equal rights under the law. His legal work throughout his career led to more protection under the law for women, children, the homeless and prisoners.

Later in his career, Marshall became the first African American to serve on the Supreme Court. He served on the court for 24 years, only retiring in 1991, when he was 81, due to poor health that included bronchitis and a heart condition that led to a pacemaker. He walked with a cane, and wore white support socks to control problematic circulation.

Marshall was born to a middle-class family in Baltimore. His first name was actually "Thoroughgood," which he shortened for the sake of convenience in writing. While his mother preferred a medical or dental career for him, he displayed an interest in law. In 1930 he applied to the University of Maryland Law School, but was denied permission due to his color. Subsequently, he went to Howard University Law School, where he graduated in 1933, first in his class and as its valedictorian.

After practicing law for some time in the Baltimore area, he joined the Baltimore branch of the NAACP and became both active and successful in obtaining more legal rights for African Americans. He served as the organization's legal director during the 1940–1961 period. During his lengthy time with the NAACP he was also asked by both the United Nations and the United Kingdom to help draft the constitutions of Ghana and Tanzania, two emerging African nations.

He became well experienced in appearing before the Supreme Court, and was known for his direct style of pleading. He represented more clients, and won more cases, before the Supreme Court than any other American—of any color.

His most crucial case came in *Brown v. the Board of Education* in 1954, which he won, thereby ending public school segregation. One of the major points of his winning argument, backed up by ample proof, was that segregation made black children feel inferior, not just during school age but for the rest of their lives. When Marshall was asked for a definition of "equal," he said, "Equal means getting the same thing, at the same time, and in the same place."

Among the measures of his increasing fame was a *Time* magazine cover in September 1955 and a children's song, "Thurgood Marshall, Mr. Civil Rights," sung to the tune of the "Ballad of Davy Crockett."

The major victory of *Brown v. the Board of Education* helped generate the Civil Rights movement in the 1960s and greater black empowerment in all fields of endeavor. Affecting a change in the law was one thing; enforcing it was another. Marshall was also effective in using the court to thwart resistance to desegregation of schools in some states.

President John F. Kennedy, overcoming opposition by racists, appointed Marshall to the U.S. Court of Appeals for the 2nd Circuit in 1961. He wrote well over 100 opinions for that court, with none overturned on appeal. Key issues upheld involved support for the rights of immigrants, the right of privacy and limiting government use of search and seizure. He was also instrumental in bringing a case involving Virginia's opposition to the Voting Rights Act of 1965 to the Supreme Court, whose subsequent decision forced Virginia to abolish its poll tax.

During 1965–67 he served as Solicitor General (the first African American to hold this position) under President Lyndon B. Johnson, who succeeded Kennedy when he was assassinated.

President Johnson then named Marshall to become a justice of the Supreme Court in 1967, where he continued his dedication to protecting the rights of Americans. Marshall was known for some of his dissents. In *San Antonio School District v. Rodriguez* he disagreed with the Court's 5 to 4 decision that the Constitution's guarantee of equal protection wasn't violated by the property tax system employed by Texas and some other states to finance public education. His 63-page opinion included a criticism of the majority of the Court "of unsupportable acquiescence in a system which deprives children in their earliest years of the chance to reach their full potential as citizens."

Another famous moment came during a 1981 case involving the death penalty, which he opposed. When then-Chief Justice William H. Rehnquist opined that perhaps an inmate's repeated use of appeals was costing the state too much money, Marshall questioned with considerable sarcasm, "It would have been cheaper to shoot him right after he was questioned, wouldn't it?"

In a case involving privacy, he ruled with the rest of the court that the government lacked the constitutional right to stop a citizen from privately reading or watching any material, including pornography. He wrote,

> If the first amendment means anything, it means that a State [Georgia in this case] has no business telling a man, sitting alone in his own house, what books he may read or what films he may watch. Our whole constitutional heritage rebels at the thought of giving government the power to control men's minds.

Marshall differed from his peers on the Court in opposing the death penalty, but sided with the majority in ruling against President Richard M. Nixon trying to stop publication of the "Pentagon Papers" (revealing Vietnam War machinations by the government) by the *New York Times* and *Washington Post.* He also was with the minority in the *Bakke* case involving affirmative action, a policy he felt was still needed to help African Americans.

Marshall came under considerable criticism for his viewpoints. Negative perceptions of his drinking (he admitted to imbibing a bit too much on occasion) didn't help. Especially damaging comments emerged in a book about the Supreme Court, *The Brethren,* co-written by Bob Woodward of Watergate fame. Many people, including fellow Supreme Court members, came to Marshall's defense and disputed the book's charges.

Marshall retired from the Supreme Court in 1991 and died in 1993 at the age of 84. His funeral was a major event, with tributes from around the world. The Thurgood Marshall College, a small liberal arts school, is part of the University of California at San Diego. There is also a Thurgood Marshall Scholarship Fund. But his most lasting legacy is easily his enormous victories in securing more civil rights for Americans, and removing legal segregation from our public schools.

One tribute came from Chief Justice Rehnquist, in reference to words above the front entrance of the Supreme Court—"Equal Justice For All"—who said, "Surely no one individual did more to make these words a reality than Thurgood Marshall."

Some of Marshall's memorable comments were:

"In recognizing the humanity of our fellow beings, we pay ourselves the highest tribute."

"Ending racial discrimination in jury selection can be accomplished only by eliminating peremptoty challenges."

"Mere access to the courthouse doors does not by itself assure a proper functioning of the adversary process."

"A child born to a black mother in a state like Mississippi has exactly the same rights as a white baby born to the wealthiest person in the U.S. It's not true, but I challenge anyone to say it is not a goal worth working for."

Dr. Jonas Salk
1914–1995
&
Dr. Albert Sabin
1906–1993

Both physicians have been celebrated worldwide for helping save millions of lives with their medical discoveries, most notably a vaccine to provide immunity against polio. Their lives mirrored each other to a considerable extent, with a strong rivalry between them.

Both developed their vaccines by building on the work of others. Salk was the first to succeed, releasing the discovery of his vaccine in 1955, but he was widely criticized for not first submitting his findings for peer review and providing insufficient credit to others who had paved the way and worked with him. Other scientists were critical of his behavior (some even referred to him as "Jonas Christ"). There was also confusion over the extent of the vaccine's effectiveness. The media hopped on the discovery story in a flurry of interviews and articles. Salk was whirled into a publicity furor he wasn't prepared to handle as his name became a household word. Even a feature film came into consideration, with none other than Marlon Brando set to play Salk.

Sabin's vaccine was released several years later. Both doctors refused to seek a patent on their discoveries. Questioned in a television interview by Ed Murrow about who holds the patent, Salk said, "Well, the people, I would say. There is no patent. Could you patent the sun?"

Salk also claimed that he didn't want his name placed by the discovery, as in "the Salk vaccine," which was a media usage. He said, "It's not the Salk vaccine. It embarrasses me with my colleagues to have it called 'Salk vaccine.'" However, the name—disseminated around the country and the world—spread and stuck.

During the trials of the vaccine, Salk turned down an award from the Albert Einstein College of Medicine on the grounds that the honor might give a premature verdict on the vaccine. Sabin's comment on the trials was, "Let us not confuse optimism with achievement."

As the vaccines were used, it was determined that Sabin's vaccine was more effective as well as convenient, though both are still used in complementary fashion, depending on the nation. Salk's vaccine, based on dead viruses to trigger the immune system, required an injection and booster shots. Less invasive, and based on live but crippled viruses, Sabin's vaccine is administered orally. In 1996 the Centers for Disease Control issued a ruling that the live vaccine would be phased out in the U.S. to eliminate any lingering problems, with the transition to the Salk vaccine completed by the start of 2000.

Both men had Eastern European roots. Salk was born in New York to an immigrant family from Poland, while Sabin was born in Bialystok, Poland but came to the U.S. at an early age. Both men opted for medical careers and then to do research.

Salk did later accept some honors. He was given the country's first Congressional Medal for Distinguished Civilian Service by President Dwight D. Eisenhower. In his acceptance speech he said, "For myself, and I will speak, too, for those whose contributions came before, but whose lot it was not to become a symbol for honor, I feel that the greatest reward for doing is the opportunity to do more."

In 1963 Salk founded the Salk Institute for Biological Studies at La Jolla near San Diego, California. Sabin started the Sabin Vaccine Institute at New Canaan, Connecticut.

"The time is drawing to a close when one can hope to find full understanding of many more disease processes through one discipline alone," Salk said about the Institute and his desire to broaden the interaction between those in the health field. "There are many viewpoints, and areas of interest, and there are differences in techniques used by the physicist, the chemist, the biologist, the physician, and the epidemiologist."

In later years, well after he was 65, Salk conducted research on multiple sclerosis and on AIDS (Acquired Immune Deficiency Syndrome). He wrote about the evolution and the philosophic implication of biological research in *Man Unfolding* (1972) and *The Survival of the Wisest* (1973). Two other books, written in his seventies, were *World*

Population & Human Values (1981) and *Anatomy of Reality: Merging of Intuition & Reason* (1983).

Meanwhile, Sabin also continued into his 80s as a medical statesman, consultant and lecturer. Known as a "courier of peace," he fought ignorance and poverty as well as disease. He was a consultant to the United States National Cancer Institute, a professor at the University of South Carolina's medical school, and then in 1984–86 become a senior expert consultant at the National Institutes of Health. Poor health forced his complete retirement in 1988. He was buried in Arlington National Cemetery.

Among Salk's quotes:

*"I have had dreams and I have had nightmares,
but I have conquered my nightmares because of my dreams."*

*"Life is an error-making and an error-correcting process,
and nature in marking man's papers will grade him for wisdom
as measured both by survival and by the quality of those who survive."*

"The reward for work well done is the opportunity to do more."

And from Sabin:

*"A scientist who is also a human being cannot rest while knowledge
which might be used to reduce suffering rests on the shelf."*

Mother Teresa
1910–1997

"If there are poor on the moon, we shall go there, too."

Called "the saint of the gutter" as well as "a saint on Earth," Mother Teresa was one of the greatest humanitarians in the 20th century. For her work in caring for the poor and the sick, primarily in India but throughout the world, she received the Nobel Peace Prize in 1979. She was beatified by the Roman Catholic Church in 2003 in the shortest process of beatification in modern Church history. Despite increasingly poor health she continued her efforts until finally relinquishing her position as head of the Missionaries of Charity just months before her death in 1997, when she was 87.

Her real name, reflecting her Albanian heritage, was Agnes Gonxha Bojaxhiu. She was born in 1910 in Skopje, in what is now Macedonia. At the age of 18 she decided to become a nun and joined the Order of the Sisters of our Lady of Loreto, based in Dublin, Ireland, where she learned English. She selected the name of Sister Teresa in a tribute to Saint Therese of Lisieux, the patron saint of missionaries.

At the end of 1928 she was sent to Darjeeling, a retreat at the base of the Himalayan Mountains in northern India, to complete her training. She took her final vows in 1937. A year later she was dispatched to Calcutta, capital of the Indian state of Bengal, where she taught history and geography at St. Mary's, a girl's school.

She continued teaching during the 1931–1948 period, while noting the misery of many Indians who lay sick and dying in the streets, until she had an epiphany in 1946 on a train back to Darjeeling to recover from a suspected bout with tuberculosis. She recounted the episode in this fashion:

> I realized that I had the call to take care of the sick and dying, the hungry, the naked, the homeless—to be God's Love in

action to the poorest of the poor. That was the beginning of the Missionaries of Charity.

Accordingly, she sought permission from the Church to establish a new Order of Sisters to help the poor and afflicted. Permission was duly granted by Pope Paul XII. She also became an Indian citizen in 1948. To further show her affinity with the downtrodden she picked as the official garment of the Missionaries of Charity simple white saris, the traditional garment of Indian women, adorned with sapphire blue bands. The new Order began its work in 1952.

In that same year Calcutta authorities granted her permission to use a portion of an abandoned temple to the Indian goddess Kali for her humanitarian mission. She founded the Kalighat Home for the Dying, which she named "Nirmal Hriday" or "Pure Heart." She and her few fellow nuns began taking dying Indians off the streets, where many slept at night, and cared for them to either save their lives or help them find work or other safe havens—or to allow them a more dignified death. An open-air school was established to teach slum children to read and to observe basic hygiene.

An orphanage was begun in 1953. In following years more such centers—which she called "tabernacles"—were established in many other Indian cities, as well as in other countries spanning five continents. Thousands of the needy have been helped since, with Mother Teresa traveling extensively despite her failing health (she had a pacemaker placed in her body due to a heart condition, among other ailments that included worsening eyesight). The first mobile clinic was launched in 1956. By the time of her death more than 4,500 sisters (as well several hundred brothers) were part of the Missionaries of Charity, serving in excess of 550 centers in over 125 countries.

A 1969 documentary, *Something Beautiful for God,* helped spread her fame.

In describing her credo, she wrote: "I see God in every human being. When I wash the leper's wounds, I feel I am nursing the Lord Himself. Is it not a beautiful experience?"

She also defined the role of her order in this fashion: "We are first of all religious; we are not social workers, not teachers, not nurses or doctors, we are religious sisters. We serve Jesus in the poor."

As far as reducing the fast tempo of her life, she said, "There will be plenty of time to rest in eternity. Here there is so much to do."

From her acceptance speech for the Nobel Prize, she said,

> I choose the poverty of our poor people. But I am grateful to receive the Nobel (Prize) in the name of the hungry, the naked, the homeless, of the crippled, of the blind, of the lepers, of all those people who feel unwanted, unloved, uncared for throughout society, people that have become a burden to the society, and are shunned by everyone.

Subsequently, she also lamented what she termed the poverty of western countries. She stated, "Around the world, not only in the poor countries, I found the poverty of the West so much more difficult to remove..."

Prize money was used to fund the Centers. In 1986, a visit to the Soviet Union led to the first time since the 1917 revolution that a religious mission was given permission to open a center in Moscow. Honorary U.S. citizenship was awarded in 1996, with Mother Teresa one of only three people to ever receive this signal honor.

As a devout Catholic, she opposed family planning/contraception programs and abortion, which led to some criticism given India's soaring population (she was even dubbed a "religious imperialist"). Mother Teresa was quite traditional and doctrinaire, always calling for obedience to the Church's doctrines. Subservience of women to men and the insistence of austerity at the Centers were other issues that drew criticism. She was also challenged on concentrating on helping the poor and destitute in their final hours, while extolling Christianity in the process, and not doing more with available resources to alleviate and eradicate poverty in Calcutta.

As far as religion, she said, "There is only one God and He is God to all; therefore it is important that everyone is seen as equal before God. I've always said we should help a Hindu become a better Hindu, a Moslem a better Moslem, a Catholic become a better Catholic."

Among her writings are two books: *A Simple Path* and *My Life for the Poor: Mother Teresa of Calcutta*.

She died in Calcutta at the age of 87. Her body was seen in an open casket by thousands, with a 21-gun salute another state tribute.

International television coverage showed dignitaries from around the world and a banner at her altar that read: "Works of love are works of peace."

On her tomb, now a shrine, the message is: "Love one another as I have loved you."

Other notable comments were:

"The hunger for love is much more difficult to remove than the hunger for bread."

"We are all pencils in the hands of God."

"Kind words can be short and easy to speak, but their echoes are truly endless."

"It is not how much we do, but how much love we put in the doing. It is not how much we give, but how much love we put in the giving."

"To God there is nothing small. The moment we have given it to God, it becomes infinite."

In her own self-description she considered herself to be

"God's pencil—a tiny bit of pencil with which He writes what He likes."

In another famous quote, she said,

"The other day I dreamed that I was at the gates of heaven. And St. Peter said, 'Go back to Earth. There are no slums here.'"

Dr. Benjamin Spock
1903–1998

"Trust yourself. You know more than you think you do."

These famous words by Dr. Benjamin Spock, one of the most trusted pediatricians in medical history, are part of the heritage stemming from his much-read and respected book, *The Common Sense Book of Baby & Child Care*. The book, which has been out in seven editions and translated into many languages, has sold more copies than any other book besides the Bible. The original paperback in 1946 sold for only 25 cents.

Dr. Spock's book was revolutionary in its time. He contradicted the prevalent advice of strictness in childrearing and advocated parents to show more flexibility and see their children as individuals. Previously, parents were instructed that picking up crying infants would only spoil them; Spock, to the contrary, argued that showing affection would make babies more secure and happy.

His book, written in a down-to-earth common sense fashion with a distinctive absence of medical terminology, was an immediate success. His name became a household word.

However, in later years, his theories—which had been widely applauded and accepted—ran into opposition. This came about especially in the 1960s, when he was accused of having helped set the stage for the so-called "Me Decade" and for generating an era of "instant gratification." Among other sobriquets he was called the "Father of Permissiveness" and termed responsible for the "Spock-marked generation of hippies." Opposition to his theories virtually became a debate that perhaps reflected the beginning or growth of cultural conflicts in the U.S. One pithy comment was that this generation was "Spocked when it should have been spanked."

In later editions of his book Spock updated the material, paying special attention to emerging issues such as single and working mothers, daycare centers, etc. He came out in support of adoption rights for gay parents, and termed the majority of computer games "a colossal waste of time." He was still working on the seventh edition when he passed away at the age of 95.

Spock, while amending his theories (making changes like using "the baby" instead of the pronoun "he"), also defended them, especially on the issue of permissiveness. He continued to argue for flexibility in parenting. "Good-hearted parents who aren't afraid to be firm when necessary can get good results with either moderate strictness or moderate permissiveness. On the other hand, a strictness that comes from harsh feelings or a permissiveness that is timid or vacillating can each lead to poor results."

In 1989 he and his second wife came out with *Spock on Spock: A Memoir of Growing Up with the Country.* At the age of 92 he wrote *A Better World for Our Children: Rebuilding American Family Values.*

He retired from his medical practice in 1967 but remained active well past his 65th birthday, veering into social and political activism in the latter decades of his life. He became an anti-nuclear, anti-Vietnam, pro-disarmament activist/pacifist and participated in demonstrations well into his 80s and 90s. His first demonstration, calling for a halt to arms testing, came in 1962 when he was nearly 60. He was arrested at the age of 65 for his anti-war activities.

He supported President John F. Kennedy in his 1960 campaign, but subsequently wrote the president to advise him, presciently as it turned out, against involvement in Vietnam. At Kennedy's request he served on a committee of doctors who supported Medicare; the program, controversial at the time, was opposed by many physicians. He also became a spokesman for the National Committee for a Sane Nuclear Policy (SANE), having warned as early as 1962 of possible dangers to children and nursing mothers by nuclear testing.

"I'm ashamed to say," Spock said, "that it took me so long to realize that politics is a crucial part of pediatrics. How else are we going to get better schools, health care for our children, and housing for their families, if not by political activity."

Spock was also subject to further arrests during demonstrations, and was even convicted at a 1968 trial. He vowed "to go on working against the war" and urged the country to "Wake up before it's too late!" Upon appeal, his conviction was overturned the following year. Overall, he was involved in protests that involved three presidents—Johnson, Nixon and Reagan—with his last arrest in 1981, when he was nearly 80. In his *A Call to Resist* manifesto in 1967 he questioned the legality of the Vietnam War and urged resistance to the draft. His FBI file ballooned.

Hardly discouraged, Spock even ran for president on the People's Party ticket in the 1972 election when was nearly 70. He garnered less than 80,000 votes; his name only appeared on the ballots in 10 states.

"I'm not allowed by my conscience to stop," Spock said. In another quote: "What's the use of physicians like myself trying to help parents bring up children healthy and happy to have them killed in such numbers for a cause that is ignoble."

A critic of society to the end of his life, Spock wrote in 1994,

When I look at our society and think of the millions of children exposed every day to its harmful effects, I am near despair. Our greatest hope is to bring up children inspired by their opportunities for being helpful and loving.

Spock was imbued with his attitude by a demanding mother. He was born in New Haven, Connecticut in 1903 as the oldest of six children, which meant he took care of some of his siblings. He went to Yale, and rowed on the university's crew team, which won a gold medal in the 1924 Olympics. He eventually graduated first in his class in 1929 from the Columbia College of Physicians and Surgeons in New York City. Unlike other pediatricians he decided to study psychoanalysis and to be analyzed himself; in the process he became greatly influenced by Freudian theories, which entered into his own writings. As Freud's theories fell into some disfavor, so has this aspect of Spock's work. But the jury, overall, is still out on his central credo of a non-authoritarian and more flexible approach to bringing up children.

A physical enthusiast, to some extent, Spock also continued being active on this front. He swam and snorkeled in the Caribbean in the late 1980s. Remarkably, in 1986 he trained for entering a rowing contest on the island of Tortola. In a field of 11, he came in eighth—at the age of 82.

Despite some severe health setbacks he recovered his strength partially, perhaps aided by a new macrobiotic diet of fish and herbs. Finally he passed way in 1998 at the age of 95.

Among Spock's many sayings:

> *"In automobile terms, the child supplies the power but the parents have to do the steering."*

> *"There are only two things a child will share willingly—communicable diseases and his mother's age."*

> *"What good mothers and fathers instinctively feel like doing for their babies is usually best after all."*

Bibliography

Aichele, Gary Jan. *Oliver Wendell Holmes.* Boston: Twayne, 1989.

Bak, Richard. *Casey Stengel: A Splendid Baseball Life.* Dallas, TX: Taylor, 1997.

Baker, Rosalie & Baker, Charles. *Ancient Greeks.* New York: Oxford, 1997.

Bar-Zahar, Michael. *Ben-Gurion: A Biography.* New York, Adama, 1978.

Bent, Silas. *Justice Oliver Wendell Holmes.* New York: Vanguard, 1932.

Beyer, Edvard. *Ibsen: The Man & His Work.* New York: Taplinger, 1980.

Bloom, Harold. *Yeats.* Broomall, PA: Chelsea House, 2001.

Bownon-Kruhn, Mary. *Margaret Mead.* Westport, CT: Greenwood, 2003.

Brian, Denis. *Einstein: A Life.* New York: Wiley, 1996.

Calder, Robert. *Willie: The Life of W. Somerset Maugham.* New York: St. Martin's Press, 1989.

Carter, Richard. *Breakthrough: The Saga of Jonas Salk.* New York: Trident, 1965.

Chamberlain, Lesley. *The Secret Artist: A Close Reading of Sigmund Freud.* New York: Seven Stories Press, 2001.

Clurman, Harold. *Ibsen.* New York: Macmillan, 1977.

Collier, James. *The Susan B. Anthony You Never Knew.* N.Y.: Children's Press, 2004.

Coolidge, Olivia. *George Bernard Shaw.* Boston: Houghton, 1968.

Cory, Daniel. *Santayana: The Later Years.* New York: Braziller, 1963.

Cotes, Peter & Cotes, Thelma Niklaus. *The Little Fellow: The Life & Works of Charles Spencer Chaplin.* New York: Citadel Press, 1951.

Craft, Robert. *Stravinsky: Glimpses of a Life.* New York: St. Martin's Press, 1992.

Splendid Seniors

Debre, Patrick. *Louis Pasteur.* Baltimore: Johns Hopkins, 2000.

de Launay, Jacques. *De Gaulle & His France.* New York: Julian, 1968.

Dils, Tracy. *Mother Teresa.* Philadelphia: Chelsea House, 2001.

Doak, Robin S. *Galileo: Astronomer & Physicist.* Minneapolis, MN: Compass Point, 2005.

Donoghue, Denis. *William B. Yeats.* New York: Ecco, 1988.

Eikhenbaum, Boris. *Tolstoi in the Seventies.* Ann Arbor, MI: Ardis, 1982.

Faurcherau, Serge. *Arp.* New York: Rizzoli, 1988.

Feingold, Mordechai. *The Newtonian Movement: Isaac Newton & the Making of Modern Culture.* New York: Oxford, 2004.

Fischer, Louis. *The Life of Mahatma Gandhi.* New York: Harper & Row, 1983.

Fox, Karen & Keck, Aries. *Einstein: A to Z.* Hoboken, NJ: Wiley, 2004.

Fox, Richard Wightman. *Reinhold Niebuhr.* Ithaca: Cornell University Press, 1996.

Fox, Stephen. *John Muir & His Legacy.* Boston: Little, Brown, 1981.

Frampton, Kenneth. *Le Corbusier.* New York: Harry N. Abrams, 2001.

Furia, Philip. *Irving Berlin: A Life in Song.* New York: Schirmer, 1943.

Gaines, Ann. *Douglas MacArthur: Brilliant General, Controversial Leader.* Berkeley Heights, NJ: Enslow Publishers, 2001.

Ganz, Arthur. *George Bernard Shaw.* New York: Grove Press, 1983.

Gay, Peter. *Freud: A Life for Our Times.* New York: Norton, 1998.

Gill, Gillian. *Mary Baker Eddy.* Reading, MA: Perseus, 1998.

Gleick, James. *Isaac Newton.* New York: Pantheon, 2003.

Gold, Arthur & Fisdale, Robert. *The Divine Sarah: The Life of Sarah Bernhard.* New York: Vintage, 1992.

Greene, Meg. *Mother Teresa: A Biography.* Westport, CT: Greenwood, 2004.

Grosvenor, Edwin & Wesson, Morgan. *Alexander Graham Bell: The Life & Times of the Man Who Invented the Telephone.* New York: Abrams, 1997.

Harsher, Benjamin. *Marc Chagall & His Times.* Stanford, CA: Stanford University Press, 2004.

Hart, Michael. *The Hundred: A Ranking of the Most Influential Persons in History.* Secaucus, NJ: Hart, 1992.

Hayman, Ronald. *Thomas Mann: A Biography.* N.Y.: Scribner, 1995.

Heilbut, Anthony. *Thomas Mann: Eros and Literature.* New York: Knopf, 1966.

Hibbard, Howard. *Michelangelo.* New York: Harper & Row, 1974.

Hibbert, Christopher. *Disraeli & His World.* New York: Scribner, 1978.

Highfield, Roger & Carter, Paul. *The Private Lives of Albert Einstein.* New York: St. Martin's Press, 1994.

Hill, Eldon. *George Bernard Shaw.* Boston: Twayne, 1978.

Hoffman, Hans. *The Theology of Reinhold Niebuhr.* New York: Scribner, 1956.

Horowitz, Joseph. *Understanding Toscanini.* New York: Knopf, 1987.

Howard, Jane, *Margaret Mead: A Life.* New York: Fawcett, 1984.

Huxtable, Ada Louise. *Frank Lloyd Wright.* Waterville, ME: Thorndike, 2005.

Isaacson, Walter. *Benjamin Franklin: An American Life.* New York: Simon & Schuster, 2003.

Israel, Paul. *Edison: A Life of Invention.* New York: Wiley, 1998.

Jablonski, Edward. *Irving Berlin: American Troubador.* New York: Holt, 1999.

Jeffares, Norman. *W.B. Yeats.* New York: Continuum, 2001.

Jenkins, Roy. *Churchill: A Biography.* New York: Farrar, Straus & Giroux, 2001.

Josephson, Matthew. *Edison: A Biography.* New York: Wiley, 1992.

Kallir, Jane. *Grandma Moses.* New York: Abrams, 2001.

Kaplan, Fred. *The Singular Mark Twain.* New York: Doubleday, 2003.

Kellogg, Charlotte. *Paderewski.* New York: Viking, 1969.

Ketchum, William. *Grandma Moses: An American Original.* New York: Smithmark, 1996.

Kick, Russ, Ed. *Abuse Your Illusions.* St. Paul, MN: The Disinformation Company, 2003.

Kirk, Connie Ann. *Mark Twain: A Biography.* Westport, CT: Greenwood, 2003.

Kluger, Jeffrey. *Splendid Solution: Jonas Salk & the Conquest of Polio.* Waterville, ME: Putnam, 2005.

Krass, Peter. *Carnegie.* New York: Wiley, 2002.

Kurzke, Herman. *Thomas Mann: Life as a Work of Art,* Princeton, NJ: Princeton University Press, 2002.

Ledwidge, Bernard. *De Gaulle.* New York: St. Martin's Press, 1982.

Lyttle, Richard. *Picasso.* New York: Atheneum, 1989.

Maier, Thomas. *Dr. Spock: An American Life.* New York, Harcourt Brace, 1998.

Manchester, William. *American Caesar: Douglas MacArthur.* New York: Little, Brown, 1978.

Mara, Wil. *Thurgood Marshall: Champion for Civil Rights.* New York: Franklin Watts, 2004.

Meltzer, Milton. *The Many Lives of Andrew Carnegie.* New York: Franklin Watts, 1997.

Meyers, Jeffrey. *Robert Frost: A Biography.* Bridgewater, NJ: Replica, 1999.

Meyers, Jeffrey. *Maugham: A Life.* New York: Knopf, 2004.

McDonald, Fiona. *Winston Churchill.* Milwaukee, WI: World Almanac Library, 2003.

McLeese, Don. *Susan B. Anthony.* Vero Beach, FL: Rourke, 2003.

Middleton, Haydn. *Frank Lloyd Wright.* Chicago: Heinemann Library, 2002.

Miracrees, Tom. *Grandma Moses.* New York: Chelsea House, 1989.

Mitford, Jessica. *The Trial of Dr. Spock.* New York, Knopf, 1969.

Morgan, Edmund. *Benjamin Franklin.* New Haven, CT: Yale University Press, 2002.

Moses, Grandma. *Grandma Moses: My Life's History.* New York: Harper & Row, 1948.

Mundt, Hannelore. *Understanding Thomas Mann.* Columbia, S.C.: University of South Carolina Press, 2004.

Oliver, Michael. *Stravinsky.* London: Phaidon, 1995.

Parini, Jay. *Robert Frost: A Life.* New York: Holt, 2000.

Pasachof, Naomi. *Alexander Graham Bell: Making Connections.* New York: Oxford, 1998.

Payne, Robert. *The Great God Pan: Biography of the Tramp Played by Charles Chaplin.* New York: Hermitage House, 1952.

Payne, Robert. *The Great Man: Winston Churchill.* New York: Coward, 1974.

Picasso, Oliver. *Picasso: The Real Family Story.* New York: Prestel, 2002.

Proctor-Gregg, Humphrey. *Beecham Remembered.* London: Duckworth, 1976.

Purcell, Sarah. *The Life & Work of Eleanor Roosevelt.* Indianapolis: Alpha, 2002.

Read, Herbert. *The Art of Jean Arp.* New York: Abrams, 1968.

Reid, Charles. *Thomas Beecham: An Independent Biography.* New York: Dutton, 1962.

Reinfeld, Fred. *The Great Dissenters.* New York: Crowell, 1959.

Richards, Simon. *Corbusier & the Concept of Self.* New Haven, CT: Yale University Press, 2003.

Sach, Harvey. *Toscanini.* Philadelphia: Lippincott, 1978.

Secrest, Meryle. *Frank Lloyd Wright: A Biography.* University of Chicago Press: Chicago, 1992.

Segovia, Andres. *Andres Segovia: An Autobiography.* New York: Macmillan, 1976.

Scodel, Ruth. *Sophocles.* Boston: Twayne, 1984.

Shea, William & Artigas, Mariano. *Galileo in Rome.* New York: Oxford, 2003.

Silverthome, Elizabeth. *Sarah Bernhardt.* New York: Chelsea House, 2004.

Singer, Irving. *George Santayana: Literary Philosopher.* New Haven, CT: Yale University Press, 2000.

Smith, Linda. *Louis Pasteur: Disease Fighter.* Springfield, NJ: Enslow, 1997.

Splendid Seniors

Spink, Kathryn. *Mother Teresa: A Complete Authorized Biography.* San Francisco: Harper & Row, 1997.

Stillman, Drake. *Galileo: Pioneer Scientist.* Toronto: Oxford, 1990.

Thomas, David. *Henrik Ibsen.* New York: Grove, 1984.

Troyat, Henri. *Tolstoyi.* New York: Grove, 2001.

True, Kelley. *Pablo Picasso: Breaking All the Rules.* New York: Grosset & Dunlap, 2002.

Ultimate Biography. New York: DK Publishing, 2002.

Vail, John. *Ben Gurion.* New York: Chelsea House, 1987.

Vasari, Giorgio. *Life of Michelangelo.* New York: Alba House, 2003.

Verhoff, Edward & Shore, Rima. *Penguin International Dictionary of Contemporary Biography.* New York: Penguin, 2001.

von Fettweiss, Yvonne & Warneck, Robert. *Mary Baker Eddy: Christian Healer.* Boston: Christian Science Publishing, 1998.

Wachhorst, Wyn. *Thomas Alva Edison.* Cambridge, MA: M.I.T. Press, 1981.
Weintraub, Stanley. *Disraeli: A Biography.* New York: Dutton, 1993.

Welton, Jude. *Marc Chagall.* New York: Watts, 2003.

White, Edward. *Oliver Wendell Holmes: Sage of the Supreme Court.* New York: Oxford, 2000.

Whitney, Sharon. *Eleanor Roosevelt.* New York: Watts, 1982.

Williams, Juan. *Thurgood Marshall: American Revolutionary.* New York: Random House, 1998.

Wolfe, Linnie. *The Life of John Muir.* Madison, WI: University of Wisconsin Press, 1945.

Wollheim, Richard. *Sigmund Freud.* New York: Viking, 1981.

Wolpert, Stanley. *Gandhi's Passion.* New York: Oxford, 2001.

Wright, David. *Frank Lloyd Wright: Visionary Architect.* Springfield, NJ: Enslow, 1999.

Zamoyski, Adam. *Paderewski,* New York: Atheneum, 1982.

About the Author

Other books by Jack Adler:

NONFICTION
There's A Bullet Hole In Your Window
Exploring Historic California
Consumer's Guide to Travel
Southern India
Travel Safety (co-authored)

FICTION
Blackmail High
Parthian Retreat

Adler and his wife, Barbro, live in Los Angeles. They have two sons. He teaches writing courses at UCLA Extension and for the Writer's Digest School.

About Pearlsong Press

Pearlsong Press is an independent publishing company dedicated to providing books and resources that entertain while expanding perspectives on the self and the world. The company was founded by Peggy Elam, Ph.D., a psychologist and former journalist.

PEARLS ARE FORMED when a piece of sand or grit or other abrasive, annoying, or even dangerous substance enters an oyster and triggers its protective response. The substance is coated with shimmering opalescent nacre ("mother of pearl"), the coats eventually building up to produce a beautiful gem. The self-healing response of the oyster thus transforms suffering into a thing of beauty.

The pearl-creating process reflects our company's desire to move outside a pathological or "disease" based model of "mental health" and "mental illness" into a more integrative and transcendent perspective on life, health, and well-being. A move out of suffering into joy.

And that, we think, is something to sing about.

PEARLSONG PRESS endorses **Health At Every Size**, an approach to health and well-being that celebrates natural diversity in body size and encourages people to stop focusing on weight (or any external measurement) in favor of listening to and respecting natural appetites for food, drink, sleep, rest, movement, and recreation.

While not every book we publish specifically promotes Health At Every Size (by, for instance, featuring fat heroines or educating readers on size acceptance), none of our books or other resources will contradict this holistic and body-positive perspective.

WE ENCOURAGE YOU to enjoy, enlarge, enlighten and enliven yourself with other Pearlsong Press books, including:

The Singing of Swans
a novel about the Divine Feminine
by Mary Saracino

Beyond Measure:
A Memoir About Short Stature & Inner Growth
by Ellen Frankel

Unconventional Means:
The Dream Down Under
by Anne Richardson Williams

Taking Up Space:
How Eating Well & Exercising Regularly Changed My Life
by Pattie Thomas, Ph.D.
with Carl Wilkerson, M.B.A.
(foreword by Paul Campos, author of
The Obesity Myth)

Romance novels and short stories featuring Big Beautiful Heroines
by Pat Ballard, the Queen of Rubenesque Romances:
Abigail's Revenge
Dangerous Curves Ahead
Wanted: One Groom
Nobody's Perfect
His Brother's Child
A Worthy Heir

FIND THESE BOOKS AND MORE at www.pearlsong.com or your favorite online or offline bookstore. Enjoy!

www.ingramcontent.com/pod-product-compliance
Lightning Source LLC
Chambersburg PA
CBHW031507270326
41930CB00006B/291